PRAISE FOR

KONG BOYS

"Equal parts travelogue, tribute to the enduring bonds of friendship, and unabashed homage to the world's most popular sport, *Kong Boys* is an illuminating, humorous, heartfelt tale of adventure, penned by one of soccer's biggest fans."

-Matthew Félix, author of *Porcelain Travels*

"A beautiful ode to the enduring power of friendship disguised as a booze-soaked, contemplative travelogue. Packed with hijinks and astute observations, *Kong Boys* is 'The Hangover' meets *A Moveable Feast.*"

-Ross Kenneth Urken, author of *Another Mother*

"A heart-warming tale of friendship and a fun romp of a travelogue which will be sure to please football fanatics everywhere."

-K.C. Finn, Readers' Favorite 5-star review

"An essential addition to the travel writing genre. This story expanded my worldview by detailing Europe from a Hong Kong perspective. It also reinforced my sense of our universal humanity through its exploration of growing up, stepping beyond one's comfort zone and the friendships that help get you there."

-Thomas Kohnstamm, author of *Do Travel Writers Go to Hell?* and *Lake City* (Instagram: @Thomas.writes)

"The exuberance of youth is ingeniously captured."

-Romuald Dzemo, Readers' Favorite 5-star review

"If this European romp doesn't prove that Gerald Yeung will do almost anything for soccer, I don't know what will. He and his band of misfits never slow down, with lots of laughs along the way."

-Larry Habegger, executive editor, Travelers' Tales

"A valuable insight into the life of the long-distance Manchester United fan. It shows how the global game matters to supporters thousands of miles away."

- Richard Jolly, Football writer for *the National, Guardian, Observer, Straits Times, Sunday Express, Daily Telegraph, FourFourTwo & Blizzard*

ALSO BY GERALD YEUNG

Wannabe Backpackers

KONG BOYS

SEVEN FRIENDS TAKE ON ELEVEN EUROPEAN
CITIES FOR THEIR THIRTIETH BIRTHDAYS

GERALD YEUNG

First edition June 2020

Cover design by Xavier Comas

ISBN 978-1-7350315-1-4 (paperback)

ISBN 978-1-7350315-0-7 (ebook)

www.geraldyeung.com

ACKNOWLEDGMENTS

I'd like to thank my family for my happy upbringing. I'm grateful that my parents, Clement, Virginia, and Goo-ma trust me to tell their story.

Very special thanks to Barbara for her eye for detail; to Liz for helping me develop the story; to Xavier for the cover of every soccer fan's dreams; and to Cassie, my campaign manager and social media consultant.

Peter, Larry, Richard, Thomas - thank you for answering a fan letter.

I am grateful to my friends who read various drafts of this book - Jackie, Vincy, Laïla, Wynne, Selina, Dionne, Vivianne and many others. You are kind, generous, and incredibly hot.

Dave, Sho, Kenny, Justin, DJ, Brian, and Lulu - thank you for being my friend.

Lastly, to Molly for her support, and always keeping it real.

To Grace, Laurie, Jena, Nancy, Amy, Mrs. Ho, and Dave's mom,

For your unconditional love, your acceptance of our antics, and your patience with Kenny's jokes about Moms.

2006

2016

CHARACTERS

(IN ORDER OF APPEARANCE)

Gerald—Engineer. Group Mom. Narrator.

Justin—MBA Student. Chef. Love Song Little Prince.

Brian—Banker. Under-the-radar high-roller.

DJ—Compliance officer. Avid photographer. Aspiring model.

Sho—Award-winning architect. Lovable little monster.

Dave—In-house lawyer. Alpha male. Textbook narcissist.

Kenny—Lawyer. Model employee. Everyone's best friend.

Lulu—Accountant. Missed the trip but good lord, can he sing.

PROLOGUE

ON JUNE 11, 2006, five twenty-year-olds from Hong Kong began their trip around the world in Lima.

Over a sumptuous seafood dinner at La Rosa Náutica, we'd painted an enamored picture of our future selves in ten years. We'd suspected that our boyband locks would be gone, and that a few gray strands would make us even more irresistible. We'd predicted that girls would come in droves for us, except for Brian, who would remain a virgin forever. We'd forecasted our net worth in the millions. On the road, we'd have swapped gruesome hostels for the Ritz-Carlton. All of Hong Kong—and, by small extension, planet Earth—would either know us or know of us thanks to our meteoric rise. Magazines would label us "debonair young men on the verge of greatness."

"In 2016," I'd said, "we'll do another trip."

We couldn't wait to celebrate our inevitable world domination.

. . .

Ten years came and went. We have fallen some way short of our lofty dreams. Reaching for an extraordinary life on pedestrian salaries, for which our bank accounts have little to show. Our stature has grown, albeit in the wrong circles and for the wrong reasons. Good girls want nothing to do with us. We still drink; we still gamble; we still stay up late.

But the past decade hasn't been a *total* failure. We all earned college degrees, a reassuring, if somewhat expected, accomplishment. Quietly, we are making small strides toward honest, respectable careers. Before starting his MBA, Justin plied his trade in Accounting and Private Equity. DJ has risen through the ranks in Compliance while also pursuing a master's degree in Law. Brian breezed through every Certified Public Accountant exam and worked his way to Senior Vice President at one of Hong Kong's major banks. Lulu, a survivor of Hong Kong's draconian accounting industry, has built a respectable resumé. I started a new life in the US as a lowly water-processing engineer, shuttling in and out of wastewater plants instead of glitzy clubs. There have been small victories. At times, we feel we've conquered Giza, even if we'd aimed for the Moon.

Despite spending most time apart, our friendship continues to blossom. We lean on each other to make light of adult hardships. And daunting as turning thirty may be, there is a trip to look forward to.

On June 18, 2016, against the backdrop of unfulfilled ambitions, failed relationships, and missed opportunities, we come good on a promise ten years in the making. Joined by three new friends in Kenny, Dave and Sho, we turn to the open road again to fulfill a lifelong dream—the UEFA

European Championship. A different continent, ten years wiser, the same childlike fearlessness.

Enough said. Let it rip.

1

DOPE — AMSTERDAM

WHEREVER YOU GO, GO WITH ALL YOUR HEART. -CONFUCIUS

"Don't go," Molly says, ten minutes from the San Francisco airport. Talk about terrible timing.

I pretend I didn't hear her.

"Well?" She turns to face me on the passenger side with raised eyebrows.

"Eyes on the road, please," I reply, hoping she can't hear the tremor in my voice. "Sorry, what did you say?"

"I know you heard me," she says.

There is no pretending now. *Why didn't I take an Uber?*

"We planned this trip ten years ago. Before I even met you!" I say, stroking her cheek to soften my tone.

She swerves into the right lane for the highway exit. This isn't the time to call her out for not using the turn signals.

"It's our dream to go to the European Championship," I continue.

She knows how much I love soccer. I watch every Manchester United game like a little fan. We never take weekend trips out of town because of my Sunday soccer game. She isn't a fan, but she goes along with it.

"But why go all the way to Europe just to watch two games?" Molly asks, her grip on the steering wheel far too loose for my liking.

"Well, it was all we could get from the ticket lottery. But it's more the experience of being there during the tournament," I reason. "Two hands on the wheel, please."

She does a fake sniffle.

"It's all an excuse to party and hit on girls in Europe."

There it is.

"No way!" I yell. "Maybe my friends. The single ones. Not me."

She scans my face to see if I am lying; I hold the steadfast gaze of an innocent man.

"So who's going?" she asks.

"Justin, Brian, and DJ. And then Dave, Sho, and Kenny will join later," I answer.

"Hmm ... I see," she mumbles. I can read the subtext—she isn't too fond of them.

For years, I had crafted a careful image of them for her. I had confided in her our secrets from primary school in Hong Kong. I had relived our shared memories from the soccer field. I had shared countless stories from our trip around the world when we were twenty. I had left out anything she might find salacious, controversial, and disrespectful. Hence, she had known them as adventurous, loyal, and loving friends who had played starring roles in my upbringing. She had been excited to meet them in person.

All that came undone last Christmas when she visited Hong Kong.

We met up with the boys at a beer pong bar. Justin was taunting a timid college kid in a heated beer pong match; DJ was busy making out with his latest love interest, completely in his own world; Brian was never one to start a conversation; and neither was she.

"I'll miss you," she says.

"Please don't make it difficult. I've got to do this," I say.

"Damn, so dramatic. You're supposed to say 'I'll miss you too,'" she jokes. "Anyways, I thought you don't even like to drink and stay up late anymore."

Pitted against my own words, I am regretting all the excuses I used not to hang out with her friends. They aren't complete lies though—ten o'clock is my bedtime these days.

"Don't worry. We're old now. I doubt we'll stay up past midnight," I say.

"Alright. Well, stay safe. Don't get hurt," she adds.

I nod.

I haven't told her about the bull run in Pamplona. I won't now.

"Aren't you glad you got here so early?" she says, ruing her Saturday plans that have been derailed by my three-hour rule.

"I don't trust Bay Area traffic," I reply.

The truth is tardiness makes me uneasy. Stressing about time is not how I like to begin my vacation.

Molly pulls up at the San Francisco airport's international terminal. I sling my backpack over my shoulder and hug her goodbye.

"Okay, I should go. Can't hang out in the drop-off zone," I say, slipping out of her embrace.

There are no cars around, but I follow rules even when no one is looking.

"Jesus, Gerald!" she groans.

"Don't forget to feed Lupe," I yell as I walk through the revolving door into the terminal.

I will miss my little puppy.

When the hotel receptionist denies my very reasonable request, I reckon it has something to do with my see-through wet T-shirt.

"Sorry, but the reservation is under Mr. Wong," he shrugs.

"Yes, I know," I plead.

I slide my phone across the counter to show him the email confirmation. After three connecting flights, a bus ride, and a long walk in the pouring rain, I have arrived in Amsterdam at my hotel. *Can I please just check in, shower, and nap before my friend arrives?*

It's barely 7 a.m. With half-lidded eyes, he sizes me up. A giant puddle pools from my rain-soaked clothes. The wheels are dangling off my suitcase after the crosstown trek on cobblestone streets. I look like the boyfriend who shows up at the door in pouring rain to win back the girl.

"Only Mr. Wong can check in to the room," he says, picking at the lint on his sweater.

I thank him and walk away.

At the other end of the lobby, I ask myself the three standard questions before I do something bad.

Am I hurting anyone? No.

Am I breaking the law? Maybe.

Will the world's overall happiness increase? Mine for sure.

The receptionist picks up on the second ring.

"Hi, my name is Ger ... mmm ... Justin Wong," I stammer. "My flight's delayed. Can my friend check in first?"

The shower is just starting to warm up when the doorbell rings. I turn off the faucet and answer in my underwear. The opening of the door lets in a rush of cool air against my bare skin. The man before me takes his sweet time to lift his eyes from his phone. He scoffs when he meets my gaze.

The first thing I notice is the roller suitcase. I don't recognize the brand, but the logo looks expensive. The owner is wearing a graphic tee under a zip-up hoodie, Lululemon sweatpants, and glasses instead of his usual contacts. The bottom half of his face is scattered with stubble from three days of no shaving. His hair is long on the top but clipped close on the sides—a popular style among famous soccer players that requires biweekly visits to the hairdresser to maintain. At the moment, his hair is matted from a sleepless night on Cathay Pacific. Justin looks disheveled and rich at the same time.

"You made it," I say.

Justin and I met in primary school in Hong Kong. Strangely, we became close friends only after leaving for boarding school—he to the UK, and I to the US. We both loved soccer and understood each other's woes of being from away from home at a young age. During those years abroad, we met up only during Christmas and summer. Through various messaging applications—ICQ, and later MSN, WhatsApp—our long-distance friendship flourished. The summer before college, Justin and I spent three weeks in Beijing training with one of the city's top high school soccer teams. It was an exclusive program, but my father knew someone who knew the coach.

"At the airport, pick up two boxes of 555 cigarettes," my father told me. "Bring it to the coach on the first day."

Every night after training, we stayed up in our service apartment slurping cup noodles and watching Hong Kong Triad movies. From the street market in Beijing, we bought matching dragon-embroidered black undershirts like the movie protagonists.

Justin flirted with the idea of attending college in the US, but he chose London School of Economics in the end. He graduated with honors in Accounting and Finance. He also minored in "social politics," otherwise known as the drama among Hong Kong students in London.

"The politics in London is crazy," he has always told me.

When we see each other, we don't hug, shake hands, or fist bump.

"Just dropped fifty euros on a fifteen-minute taxi ride," he says as he enters our hotel room. "Amsterdam *bay-gao* expensive."

Bay-gao (比較) is Cantonese for "relatively." We use it in a sarcastic sense.

"I took the bus. Only five euros. Nice Harry Potter glasses," I reply.

I like the vibe here in Amsterdam. People dress well without being pretentious. No prep school boys in loud colors. No meathead bros in small tees. No obnoxious haircuts clamoring for attention. Everyone is happy in their own skin.

Our first order of business is to decide whether or not we will smoke weed.

Leading up to the trip, Justin has asked me that question several times.

"I don't know. I'm indifferent. Let's decide later."

Though never a smoker myself, living in the US has changed my perception of marijuana. On the one hand, I know it's not good for you, at least when compared to exercise or fish oil. I once met a guy at a five-dollar Blackjack table in a small town in Nevada. His faded leather jacket reeked of smoke. He told us, without being asked, that he grew and distributed marijuana for a living.

"Weed is actually good for you," he preached, laying down two crumbled hundred-dollar bills before the dealer. "Before twenty-one, THC can harm your brain. But after twenty-one, smoking actually *helps* brain cell growth."

I looked him in the eye for five seconds, then slowly scanned the rest of the table for someone to call bullshit.

Believers will stand by its medical merits, but most people still smoke to get high. I have no issue with smokers, but personally I stay away from chemicals. I don't even take ibuprofen. Some people would call me au naturel.

On the other hand, marijuana's pervasiveness today has desensitized my aversion. In Asia, cigarettes are more socially acceptable than marijuana. In the US, it is almost the other way around. Most states in the US have legalized medical or even recreational cannabis use. It's almost no different to me than tobacco. In fact, cigarettes and I are mortal enemies; weed is my peaceful neighbor. When I was growing up in Hong Kong, we were preached that only bad people do drugs. I have come to learn this isn't always the case. Is President Obama a bad person?

But in Asia, cannabis is no joke. Marijuana is mentioned in the same breath as cocaine and heroin. When you fly into Taipei, they always remind you that drug trafficking is punishable by death.

But that doesn't mean Justin isn't curious. After all, he is a bucket list person. Moral dilemma notwithstanding, marijuana, in a risk-free setting in Amsterdam, is on the list.

Seeing his struggle, I do what best friends do.

"Alright, let's smoke," I declare, absolving him from the guilt.

We find the nearest "coffee shop." I walk in like I own the place.

"Good day sir, we would like to smoke weed," I announce, trying not to sound like a rookie.

The owner sizes us up. "A joint or roll yourself?"

"A joint, please."

"Mixed with tobacco?"

"Nah, just weed."

Justin nudges me.

"Wait, we're doing it straight up?" he mumbles.

"Hell yeah. Tobacco is bad for you."

The store owner murmurs to his staff in Dutch.

"Smoke slowly," he says as he hands over the goods.

I slide a five-euro note across the table, signaling I have had enough of his attitude.

"Hey," Justin mumbles, "can we have a beer first?"

There's a bar across the street.

"Hi, what's the strongest beer on tap?" I ask the bartender.

He points to the Brand IPA.

"Two pints please."

I take a picture of the joint next to our beers and send it to our friends. The joint is an artifact of beauty. Cannabis is wrapped within a sheet white cone, the rolling paper cut with machine precision. The mouthpiece filter ensures maximum pleasure and minimum harm. The joint is fitted inside a plastic test tube tapered to its exact dimensions. Even for someone who doesn't smoke, I can appreciate the artistry.

"Drink up!"

We clink our glasses. I take a big gulp; Justin just wets his lips.

"Ready?" I ask.

He's not ready.

Ten minutes in.

"You know what I become when I drink, right?" Justin breaks his silence. "I worry weed will take me to the next level."

Justin is a violent drunk. Alcohol unleashes his WWE fantasies. You are not his real friend until you've had a taste of his Rock Bottom.

"I think weed will actually mellow you down," I say.

As he asks for more time to think it through, I flip through a newspaper someone left behind and find this ridiculous ad.

"This couple is offering their place for couch surfers," I begin reading the ad aloud to Justin.

– We are David (Dutch, 50) and Steve (American, 39)
– We are a gay couple, but you don't have to be gay to stay here. Just be cool with it :-)
– We are nudists, which means we are usually naked at home
– If you stay with us, you will be naked inside our studio as well. No exceptions and no sexual intentions, though 'sex' is not a dirty word in our house. IMPOR-TANT: please state clearly in your request that you are fine with being naked. Requests that do not mention that will get declined automatically.

– We host guys only

– We live in a studio, so there's not much privacy, but you will have your own bed in a separate corner of the apartment

– No fake profile names, no faceless pics, low-res pic or no pic at all.

"Hahahaha," Justin laughs.

"I'm sending it to my mom with the caption '*Arrived in Amsterdam needing a place to sleep. Found this nice couple*.'"

Twenty minutes in.

Beer half gone. Some people decide to rob banks in less time than this.

Justin fires off an avalanche of texts to Vincy, his girl-friend, presumably on the forbidden fruit he is about to taste.

I decide to tell Justin a story.

"I once knew a German girl, Andrea. She had done almost every drug—acid, MDMA, Molly, marijuana ... you name it. So I asked her where it had all begun. She said when she was traveling in Australia, she and a few hippy friends found this rundown house and decided to crash it. In there, her friends introduced her to a whole bunch of drugs. Then the cops showed up."

"Shit, did they get in trouble?" Justin asks.

"No! She said since the owner didn't really care, the cops couldn't do anything about it."

Justin starts laughing.

"She breaks onto private property to do drugs, and somehow people turn a blind eye. Are you kidding me?" I scream.

Thirty minutes in.

For a narcissist like Justin, he must be aware that this inde-cision is very unattractive.

Your boyfriend (shaking my head), I text Vincy.

Forty minutes in.

In our twenties, Long-lun, our codename for Long Island Iced Teas, gave us strength to talk to girls. At thirty, IPAs soon will light Justin's first joint. What would we do without alcohol?

Fifty minutes in.

"Don't you find it ironic that the front of your shirt says 'Dope?'" I scoff, astonished it has taken me all morning to spot the irony.

He laughs a helpless laugh. "The problem is weed is too accessible, man. If I like it, I'll be hooked."

I signal for another beer and leave him to settle his own conflict.

One hour in.

I have many choice words for Justin, none of which can be shared here.

One hour fifteen minutes in.

"If I had recorded all this on time lapse, we would probably see your beard grow."

One hour twenty-five minutes in.

"Okay, I'm ready," Justin declares with more flair than Lebron James's infamous "The Decision."

"Okay, let's do it." I have fallen asleep at the table. For a moment, I thought I would die of old age in this bar.

"Wait, wait, let's go back across the street to the coffee shop. It's more authentic that way."

It takes every ounce of my self-restraint not to punch him in the face.

The coffee shop has emptied out. Only a young couple sits outside with their luggage. I doubt they debated an hour before puffing away.

And so we light it up.

We pass the joint back and forth like two kindred hearts. I feel like the proverbial bad friend holding Justin's hand as we venture into the world of narcotics. I don't smoke, but I find marijuana aromatic. It brings back memories of my college fraternity house. Yes, I also subscribe to *Playboy* for the articles.

We notice no change after five minutes.

"When are you supposed to feel something?" I ask the shopkeeper.

"Mmm ..." she looks at her watch, "right about ... now!"

We carry on, keeping conversation to a minimum in search of the first sign of "high."

"Bro, have you ever seen the way you smoke?" he asks.

"No, I don't smoke. Remember?"

"When you inhale, you look like a drag queen."

"Good to know."

"Also, you're not inhaling hard enough. No wonder you never got high."

I have smoked twice in my life. The first time I split a joint in a fraternity house basement in Montreal. The second time was at our own fraternity library. I was elected assistant house manager, and tradition required that I take a hit off a five-foot bong. Both times I coughed my lungs out but felt nothing.

"You smoked before?" I ask.

"Cigarettes when I was sixteen. I did it for six months for fun."

Yeah right. I'm sure he did it for the looks, and to pick up college girls.

We burn through another joint. I walk out of the coffee shop sober as a priest. For a brief while, there was a faint tingling in my legs, but the hysterical laughter I was longing for never arrived. Even humming to Bob Marley's "Three Little Birds" fails to unlock its potency.

"I'm not feeling shit," Justin says.

"Me neither."

After our unsuccessful attempt to get high, we walk to a restaurant Justin has earmarked from his research. Pancakes Amsterdam is famous for its authentic sugary and savory Dutch pancakes.

"Okay, I'll order for both of us," Justin says, pulling up his notes.

These pancakes are huge, the size of a dinner plate. First to arrive is a bacon, mushroom, and pepper pancake.

"It tastes like a creamier version of *choy-bo-chao-dan* (菜脯炒蛋)," I say, referring to the Chinese omelette with preserved turnip my grandma likes to make. It is good and hearty but not remarkable.

"Egg and pancakes are completely different things," Justin says. "I brought you here to eat authentic Dutch food and all you are thinking is *choy-bo-chao-dan*."

The second dish looks more promising— a crisp, buttery pancake, with red strawberry jam swirls all around and three thick blocks of brie melted on top. You can never go wrong with melted brie.

I take a bite. I pause and look over to Justin.

"Oh my god!"

The richness of flavors catches me completely by surprise.

The ingredients complement each other perfectly. It is a dish to die for, but you don't want to eat it every day.

Over Dutch pancakes, Justin and I catch up on life. I tell him about my puppy Lupe. He mentions an ex-girlfriend competing for this year's Miss Hong Kong.

"How do you feel about that?" I ask.

His exaggerated eye roll says it all.

After college Justin returned to Hong Kong and became something of a socialite, making friends and frenemies across many circles. Meanwhile, my first job brought me to suburban Upstate New York before a later move to California. We are as different in many ways as we are similar in others.

"Are the boys excited to come?" I ask, referring to Brian, DJ, Sho, Dave, and Kenny, who will be joining us soon.

"Em ... yeah," he says, his tone suggesting that I've asked a stupid question.

I'm excited to see them too.

After three days in Amsterdam, Justin and I will head to Lille to watch our first European Championship group stage game. Then our journey continues in France where Brian and DJ will join up in Paris. We four will rent a car for a whirlwind tour of Lyon, Monaco, and Saint-Tropez. In Marseille, Kenny, Dave, and Sho will join the group for the Quarter-Final match. All seven of us will travel Barcelona, Ibiza, Pamplona, and Madrid for an epic finale. I get goosebumps just thinking about it.

In an ultimate high-risk, low-reward move, I also invited my family to various portions of the trip.

"So your mom is really joining us?" Justin asks. "You sure you want her to see us in beast mode?"

"Obviously not the drinking and clubbing," I say. "We have extra tickets to the Quarter-Final in Marseille so I asked her."

"What about your aunt and cousin? Don't they live in the US?" he asks.

Our plan is to spend four epic nights in Ibiza. But because Ibiza villas are rented by the week, it would mean letting three nights go to waste. So I invited my mom, my brother Clement, my aunt, and my cousin Virginia to stay there for the remainder of the week. They were excited about the idea and planned a mini European getaway around it.

"My aunt took care of me during boarding school and college," I reason.

Every semester, she drove me to and from school. When I visited her house during breaks, she did my laundry and cooked. I wanted to do something nice for her.

Justin laughs.

"You're crazy. They're going to see a side of us you don't want them to see."

He's right. It will either turn out fine, or into a complete disaster.

Justin and I finish lunch and try to decide where to go next.

"Let's see," I say, carefully unfolding the rain-soaked map I picked up from the hotel this morning.

It is a map of Amsterdam annotated with backpacker essentials — museums, budget restaurants, train stops, Internet cafes, open-air stages, and, my favorite, "doing nothing hangout spots." The Red Light District is marked by a red-light-bulb symbol. The logo for coffee shop is a cannabis leaf interlaid over a joint. I have circled a few must-gos:

Heineken Experience, Sex Museum, Erotic Museum, and Hash Museum.

"Let's get some sightseeing out of the way," I say.

It hasn't stopped raining since we left the hotel this morning. We watch cars try to park along the canal. There is no curb; drivers are one small mistake away from a plunge and a Bond-like vehicle escape underwater. The mere sight makes my heart race.

We walk past the Amstel, a river more famous for the things named after it. Amstel beer, produced from Amstel water, is enjoyed around the world. Even the city of Amsterdam has taken its name from the river. Every day, the Amstel turns a shade greener from jealousy.

After a long walk in the rain, we arrive at the Sex Museum. I learn, among other things, the evolution of condoms. One of the exhibits is a machine that inflates condoms through the ages, from ancient ones that look thicker than jeans, to the modern rubbery kind.

"Science has come a long way," I say, pressing that button again and again.

Who would have thought that watching condoms inflate can be so therapeutic? If my mom were here, she would ask me to stop.

Next up is Red Light Secrets, also known as the Museum of Prostitution.

Prostitution in Amsterdam has Napoleon to thank for its genesis. In the old days, Amsterdam was a trading port frequented by sailors hungry for "entertainment." When the French invaded the Netherlands in 1795, they legalized prostitution. All sex workers were required to register and conduct twice-weekly testing amidst the rampant crisis of sexually transmitted diseases. Registered prostitutes were given a red card that served as a work permit. If found to be infected, their red cards would be taken away until they recover. Today there are three hundred *peeskamers* in the Red Light District where sex workers earn their daily bread. These are glass-front booths where sex workers attract customers and do their thing. According to the museum, whatever you are into, there is someone for your needs.

I have always believed in an ancient Chinese saying that there is dignity in every profession, a sentiment that is echoed by the curators of this museum. The museum portrays prostitution as an important and serious business; sex workers should be treated with respect. In one room, visitors get a taste of what it feels like to stand inside a *peeskamer*. Disgusting men try to flirt with you. At times, angry purists quote scripture to disparage you. In the worst case, drunk, violent men can harm you. These girls have families, too.

When we leave the museum, sheets of rain pummel Amsterdam and bring an instant chill to the air.

"Let's go home and take a nap," a jet-lagged Justin suggests. I concur.

"So Vincy is a good girlfriend and all," Justin says as we sprint through the rain, "but she knows nothing about soccer."

"How so?" I ask.

"The other day, it started raining on my way to a soccer game. She was like 'oh my god, you're still gonna play? What if your head gets wet?' I was like, 'err...should I hold an umbrella on the field then?'"

I fall asleep the second we get back to the room. Justin

can't sleep for some reason, so he stays up to do food research. Before his MBA, Justin spent four years in private equity. He moved to Shenzhen for the job, but spent most days on the road, a stint that exposed him to a multitude of regional Chinese cuisine. He became something of a gourmet, much to the detriment of his waistline.

"We're eating Indonesian tonight," he says when I wake up.

In the 1800s, Indonesia, or the former Dutch East Indies, was a colony of Netherlands. The Dutch in those days often entertained out-of-town guests to show off the abundance of their colony. This was how rijsttafel, which literally means "rice table," came about. Thanks to their opulence, Justin and I get to sample through twenty Indonesian dishes.

For dessert we have England versus Slovakia. At an empty bar we sit through a boring first half. The only thing worth noting is the condition of the bar's bathroom.

"Yo, don't use the bathroom," Justin warns, moving his arms in fly-swatting motion. *"Bay-gao* dirty. Lots of flies and stuff in there."

Nothing is happening at this bar. We decide to watch the second half somewhere else. We find a "coffee shop" across the street. A guy stands by the entrance like a statue. He looks like N!xau from *The Gods Must Be Crazy*; he is completely stoned. A sign on the wall reads: "Weed yes, Tobacco no." We've come to the right place.

We smoke the customary joint to no effect. All told, we have squandered twenty euros on drugs with nothing to show for.

"Time to take it to the next level." I stand up and move toward the counter.

I buy a full gram of Buddha Cheese and ask three backpackers from England to teach me how to roll a joint. I cringe every time they ask me if I want to smoke a fag.

"That word is frowned upon in the United States these days, even if you're referring to a cigarette," I tell them, disgusted at myself for sounding like a mom. I've also learned having gay friends doesn't give you the right to use gay slurs.

I take an instant interest to our three new British friends. Tom is a drama major and looks head-to-toe classic artist—shaggy hair, accessories, tattoos. His girlfriend Judy can't keep her hands off him. Then there's Rory in the corner. He is a heavyset Brit, perhaps a tad greasy for most people's liking, but he carries an air of indifference I find halfway charming. With a big fat joint between his lips, he ignores all attempts at conversation. I can sit there all day and watch Rory roll joints with the precision of a watchmaker.

I hardly pay any attention to the game on TV, which is just as well—the teams play out a goalless draw.

A gram is a lot of weed. We roll five, six joints and smoke them all. How much THC we actually consumed is up for debate as we can't seem to get our joints to light. More often than not, the whole joint goes up in smoke in seconds.

"I feel all we've been smoking is the rolling paper," Justin mutters through a long coughing fit. We didn't get high, but not for the lack of trying. I am both disappointed and happy with the outcome.

"Now I can say I've done it and it does nothing for me," Justin gushes.

Next stop—heroin.

Just kidding.

2

HUNGRY AGAIN — AMSTERDAM

AGE IS SOMETHING THAT DOESN'T MATTER, UNLESS YOU ARE A
CHEESE. –LUIS BUÑUEL

I WAKE up to the sound of spirited WWE commentary.

"What time is it?" I ask, still groggy.

"Six," Justin says, his eyes glued to the wrestling reruns on his laptop.

I look out the window and see heavy downpour. I crash back to bed.

When I wake up again, it's already noon. There are over a hundred WhatsApp messages on my phone. I sit up in bed and start scrolling through them.

My roommate wants to borrow my laundry detergent.

Go ahead, I reply.

My other group of Hong Kong friends are organizing a soccer game this Saturday.

Ignore.

My mom is asking me how my trip is going.

Good, I reply.

Want me to book anything? she asks.

Yes. Dinner. Marseille. June 29. Justin birthday, I write.

Birthday cake too? she asks.

Cake ok. Talk later.

"Wow, eighty messages in our trip group chat," I say to Justin.

We started this group a while back for planning, but the current discussion has nothing to do with where to eat, where to play, or what to bring; it is all about sports gambling.

When Hong Kong legalized soccer gambling in 2003, a whole generation of gamblers was born. We are the poster children of that generation. It has changed the way many people watch the game. Gambling makes lesser known teams worth following. Gambling gives meaning to meaningless statistics like corner kick count. When you have money on the line but the results don't go your way, you always suspect that the games are fixed.

A few weeks before the trip, we decided to start a sports betting fund.

"Just to make the Euro games more interesting," Brian said. "Maybe we can win back the plane tickets."

We all had different expectations. Sho, Brian, and Justin eyed handsome returns. DJ was happy to break even. Kenny and I expected to lose it all. Dave *wanted* to lose it all just to say, "I told you so." Though everyone understood that an individual's gambling budget was determined by his financial situation and manhood, it didn't stop us from judging DJ and Dave for limping in with just half the suggested amount. We handed the key of our sizable war chest to Brian and Sho, the trigger-happy duo who couldn't wait to get started.

"Wait, isn't the money supposed to be for betting during the trip? You guys will lose it all before we start!" Justin protested.

"What if we doubled up before we start?" Brian said, with

the self-confidence of Christopher Columbus. This was the same Brian who raised baby hamsters with me in our youth.

We decided to test the water in the tournament opener between France and Romania. Brian and Sho spent all day doing research. They felt that France would grind out a narrow win, but wouldn't actually commit to action. Both money and bragging rights were at stake.

"It's better to buy in-game," Brian explained in the group chat. "Better odds. And you need to get a feel of the game flow first."

"Brian, you're out of control with your gambling. Game flow my ass," I replied, cracking up as I read this in my office. But deep down I trusted him. He is a sneaky genius both book smart and street smart. But you wouldn't know because he doesn't gloat.

Brian scoffed. "You can quote me after I'm done doubling your ante."

They stayed up till 3 a.m. in Hong Kong for the tournament kickoff.

"How's the game flow, Brian?" Sho asked in the group chat and added a sarcastic smile emoji.

"Fast. Lots of long ball," Brian replied. I pictured him with multiple screens open and crunching numbers as he watched.

We bet for a first-half tie. It was noon in California. I followed the game on and off at my office, maintaining an emotional distance in case we lost. As the game approached the forty-five-minute mark still scoreless, I gave in and turned on the live stream. My eyes were glued to the screen as I scarfed down my lunch turkey burger. Time stood still in the final minutes of the first half. When Romania cleared a

French attack deep into stoppage time, the whistle blew for half. The score was 0–0.

We won.

Relief washed over me. Few things in life offer the catharsis of winning money.

Brian immediately placed a second bet.

"Brian's so *lawng*," Sho said. *Lawng* (狼), the Cantonese word for "wolves," is used to describe aggressive pursuit, typically for driving, playing the stock market, hitting on girls, and, of course, gambling.

What a long way we've come. Ten years ago, we were sweating over fifty-dollar roulette bets in Buenos Aires. Here we were now dropping thousands like it's monopoly money.

The second half began. It took only twenty minutes for Olivier Giroud to break the deadlock. He rose to a center forward's header, the kind of goal I had always dreamed of scoring. Romania struck back immediately through a penalty kick. The nail-biter was decided by a journeyman whose early stint at FC Nantes had required part-timing at a clothing store to supplement his apprentice income. Dimitri Payet walked off the field to a standing ovation in stoppage time, holding back his tears. His spectacular goal had lifted an entire nation and penned a glorious chapter to his legacy.

What a story. What a game.

As for us, we were up 20 percent. Not bad for testing the water.

After going through our WhatsApp messages, Justin and I get dressed and head down to the subway. We head to the street food market at De Pijp, which means "The Pipe." Built in the nineteenth century to ease overpopulation in Jordaan, De Pijp has since transformed from a working-class neighborhood into the hip cultural melting pot today. It is home to the famous Albert Cuyp Market that sells bargain clothes, antique furniture, and iPad covers. Think Women's Street in Hong Kong. We come for the food.

"Okay," Justin pulls up a list on his phone, "first up is fresh hot *stroopwafel*."

Originated from the Gouda region of the Netherlands, *stroopwafel* is made with two thin layers of baked dough sandwiching a delicious syrup paste. Working behind the waffle stand is a middle-aged man donning a pristine white chef coat and red scarf.

"Somehow he reminds me of a less creepy version of Colonel Sanders," I say.

"Who?" Justin asks.

"The KFC guy."

Standing in line pelted by the rain, we watch admirers from all around the world bite into their *stroopwafel* to instant gratification. The Japanese, the Brits, the South Africans...one after another we watch as their eyes glow in great satisfaction and they whisper to their friends.

"This guy's like a miracle doctor," I say.

When we get to the front of the line, we place the exact change on the counter and watch the magic unfold. The chef places a lump of dough on the waffle maker and presses down the cover. Exactly thirty seconds later, a thin piece of waffle in a perfect circle is formed. He splits it open like a hamburger bun and spreads syrup in between.

"*Dank je.*" He wraps the *stroopwafel* on a napkin and hands it over with a smile.

It is well worth the wait—the waffle melts in your mouth to an amalgamation of warmth, softness and sweetness. I would go back for seconds if it weren't for the long line.

Next on Justin's list is soused herring. Herring is a forage fish the length of a man's hand. They swim in schools and are best caught in the North Sea summer when their body oil content is at the highest. Soused herring, a Dutch favorite, is prepared by soaking raw herring in a mild vinegar. Most places serve it on a bun with mayonnaise, pickle, and chopped onion.

It is love at first bite.

I want to hoard all the herrings in the world to myself and keep it a secret. I know that once Hong Kong people get a taste, they will eat them to extinction. It is that good.

We go back for more.

"I think I can skip my fish oil pills for a few days," I tell Justin.

All told, we end the day on five servings of herrings each.

The street food serves as the perfect build up to the high-light of our day—the Heineken Experience. Built in 1867 as Heineken's first brewery, this historic building was repurposed as the company museum in 1991.

The story began in 1864 when twenty-two-year-old Gerard Adriaan Heineken bought a brewery. He founded the company under the mantra "I have set myself the task of continuing this business with the utmost effort and painstaking care and will leave no remedy untried to persist in supplying the best-quality beer in the long term."

Not the most original vision perhaps, but at least he took the time to write it down.

The original paper on which these words are transcribed is preserved behind a glass case in the museum.

"He bought a brewery at twenty-two? Must have rich parents," Justin comments.

"I was just about to say that."

When introduced to people who have achieved success at a young age, we are always dying to know if they come from money. Who likes to acknowledge other people's superior talent when you can attribute their success to rich parents?

Rich parents or not, Gerard took his break and ran with it. Under the Heineken family's leadership, Heineken beer has grown into a global sensation. Today, it is one of the most consumed beers *and* one of the most recognized brands in the world.

Next, we hop onto a simulator ride on a moving platform to learn about the brewing process.

Here is beer making for dummies:

Step 1: Turn barley into malt. Google for details.

Step 2: Mill the grain to crack open the husk.

Step 3: Cook the cracked grain in hot water into a thick and sweet wort. Heineken uses purified water to ensure taste consistency around the world. The cooked barley in Heineken Museum is the smell of heaven. I can stay in that room all day.

Step 4: Add hops. These are small grains that smell like feet. They give beer its bitterness.

Step 5: Aerate the wort and add yeast for fermentation. Beer math: Yeast eats sugar to make ethanol.

Step 6: Filter and package.

At long last, we arrive at the tasting room.

"We have an official way of drinking a Heineken," the young tasting master announces. "Stand tall, chest out and slightly arrogant. You're drinking the best beer in the world, after all."

Give that girl a raise.

"Tilt your glass aggressively and take big gulps. This way, you can enjoy the golden lager and not the top foam," she says, taking a hearty gulp in the correct form.

She explains the science behind it—the foam layer prevents carbon dioxide from escaping the beverage.

"Shit, I didn't know that," I say.

I have always considered the froth to be a nuisance, something you want to get rid of it. A brother at my fraternity once taught me a trick to dissolve the foam.

"Swipe your fingertip across your cheek, then stir the foam with your finger. The grease will dissolve it quickly," he said.

I have shown that trick to everyone I know. How many beers have I drunk incorrectly over the years?

A ferocious rain breaks out just as we are leaving the museum. We scramble for shelter, looking for anywhere interesting to pass the time. There's the Rijksmuseum dedicated to arts and history. Pass. It is too late in the day to go into Van Gogh Museum now. Stedelijk Museum on contemporary art holds little appeal to us. We aren't desperate enough for the Diamond Museum yet.

"Yo, let's eat here," Justin says.

I turn around and see Justin enter a Vietnamese restaurant.

"For real?" I ask.

It is barely 5 p.m. The rain has stopped, so he isn't settling for shelter. This deserted dingy restaurant feels neither authentic nor remarkable. I'm not picky when it comes to food, but even I feel we could have shopped around a bit more. But when a Dutch-Vietnamese version of Hong Kong pop star Fiona Sit comes to take our order, I know what's up.

I flash a smile at Justin; he smiles right back.

"So how long can you go without Chinese food?" Justin asks, slurping down his pho.

It's a strange question.

"I don't know. I've never thought about that."

"What? You've become a white person, man. Three, four days is my limit. After that, I must have Chinese food."

"Are you counting this as Chinese food?" I ask.

"Mmm...loosely," Justin replies.

"Well, eat up now because I doubt they have Chinese food in Lille tomorrow," I say.

We both order pho, a Vietnamese noodle soup served with basil leaves, bean sprouts, hot chili and thin slices of beef.

We hold our breath and stare as "Fiona" brings our noodles, sets them on the table, and walks away.

"She didn't give us enough fixings for the pho," Justin complains.

"Hey, you gonna eat those bean sprouts? Can I have them?" Beans sprouts are my single favorite food.

"Help yourself. Also, do you know that when you eat pho, you'll be hungry again in a couple hours? I learned that when I was working in China."

After dinner, we stroll around the neighborhood. I want to send myself a postcard. This is a travel ritual I started ten years ago at the height of my narcissism. Today, I have a shoebox full of postcards from all around the world, sent from me to me. My family remains undecided on what to make of these "Dear Gerald" mail that pops up every now and then. When I go through them once in a while, I cringe at the things I wrote back in the day. In a way, these postcards are my travel diary, and snapshots of my mental health at different junctions of my life.

Justin decides he'll write a postcard to his girlfriend.

"Why are you sending it in an envelope?" I ask.

"So her family can't read it."

I raise my eyebrows.

"Now I'm really curious what you're writing."

I've never seen Justin so cautious in a relationship. He must be really scared of this girl or absolutely in love with her.

Half an hour after our pho dinner, Justin is hungry again. We find our way to a cheese shop. The Netherlands is the biggest cheese exporter in the world. Six hundred and fifty million kilograms of cheese are produced here per year. An average Dutch consumes 14.3 kilos annually. There seems to be a cheese store around every corner. The smell of a refrigerated barnyard attacks my nostrils the moment we step in. As cheese ages, its flavors intensify. This store specializes in Gouda of all flavors—pesto, truffle, garlic and dozens more. After Justin annihilates the free samples, we walk out without buying anything.

On our way back to the subway, Justin makes another detour to a Belgian waffle place in Chinatown.

"I hate being hungry around 10 p.m.," he says preemptively.

"Can't you just sleep it off?" I ask, amused by the specificity of his statement.

"No, I can't sleep if I'm hungry."

"That explains your weight," I insinuate, with Nutella all over my face.

We make it back to our room in time for the start of Spain versus Croatia. Spain is looking for a statement win; a Croatian victory will ensure first place in the group.

We have a lot riding on this game too. A draw or better for Spain will give us a chance of seeing them at the Quarter-Final in Marseille.

Things get off to a good start. Álvaro Morata applies a simple tap-in within seven minutes to cap off a sublime team move by Spain. Without talisman Luca Modrić, Croatia leans on Ivan Perišić to turn the game around. First, he supplies the cross that sets up Croatia's equalizer just before halftime. Then, at the eighty-seventh minute, he pounces on Spain's questionable marking for the winner.

Spain's captain Sergio Ramos plays starring roles in two turning points of the game. First, he affords Kalinić acres of space for the equalizer. Later, when Spain is gifted a penalty kick on the seventy-second minute, Ramos of all people steps up. My stomach lurches.

"*Ng-hai-ma?* (唔係嗎)" I snap, holding my head in disbelief. The phrase translates to "for real?" in Cantonese. With money on the line, Ramos is not who I want to take the kick.

Conventional wisdom says give it to the regular penalty kicker at club level, which would make Fàbregas (Chelsea) the preferred choice.

"He's gonna miss," Justin whimpers, holding his breath.

Ramos begins his run up. Justin and I can barely watch.

He smashes it waist height to the center. Croatian keeper Subašić palms it away before his teammate denies Silva's follow up.

Riding the momentum of the penalty save, Croatia goes on to complete the comeback. They are the deserved winners.

Goodbye our chances of seeing Spain.

At the final whistle, Justin and I stare at the TV at a complete loss for words as they replay the penalty kick from every angle.

"You go to bed first. I can't sleep," Justin says.

He pulls out his laptop and drowns his sorrows in WWE.

3

BOYS IN GREEN—LILLE

IF YOU'RE IRISH, IT DOESN'T MATTER WHERE YOU GO—YOU'LL
FIND FAMILY. –VICTORIA SMURFIT

FOR EVERY MESSI AND RONALDO, there are millions of broken soccer dreams.

Growing up, I wanted nothing more than to play for Manchester United. Posters of Giggs and Beckham covered my childhood bedroom walls. Captain Tsubasa comic books and soccer biographies lined my bookshelves. I moved around the apartment always dribbling a soccer ball, evading chairs and tables standing in as imaginary defenders. All day I dreamed about soccer.

I never stood a chance, but I allowed myself to believe in miracles even into my twenties. If the uncounted hours spent warming the bench were life's way of insinuating the need for a plan B, I didn't listen. In college, I traveled with the team across states for tournaments where I didn't see a single minute on the field. While my non-soccer friends spent their weekends partying and sleeping in, I stayed at cheap motels and stood on the muddy sideline in the cold rain. I saw this as a test of character, safe in the knowledge that my time would come.

It never did.

There were no injuries or bad coaches to blame. I simply wasn't good enough.

Though perseverance didn't propel me past greater talents the way I had expected, it armed me with a self-belief for other avenues in life. That my soccer dreams didn't come to fruition never diminished my love for the game.

For the time I have spent playing, watching, reading and dreaming about soccer, I have never attended a major international tournament. My mother once offered to take me to the 1998 World Cup in France, but it would have cost a fortune that I didn't feel I'd earned.

Now on my own dime, Justin and I board the train to Lille for the European Championship showdown between Ireland and Italy.

At 7:30 a.m., scores of Irish fans have already taken over the Amsterdam train station, chanting and drinking Heineken. With fourteen hours till kickoff, do they have the stamina to pull through? This is soccer nirvana, the reason why fans like us travel from afar to experience.

There's only one problem—I am wearing the wrong color.

I stand out as the lone blue speck in a sea of green; the "#7 Del Piero" print tingles on my back like a Scarlet Letter.

"Bro, be careful," Justin cautions. "Don't do something stupid."

We acquired our match tickets through the FIFA lottery system a year ago. With the qualifiers still in progress and the groups yet to be decided, we submitted our bids based only on locations and dates. In the end, we got two sets of tickets — eight seats at the Quarter-Final game in Marseille, and a pair for Justin and me to attend a group stage game in Lille. I couldn't have wished for a better draw than Italy versus Ireland.

I became an Italian fan watching the Euro 2000 Semi-Final when ten-man Italy defeated a red-hot Holland in, of all places, Amsterdam. Doing their best impersonation of the three hundred Spartans, Italy defended as if Rome itself were under siege. Even flair attackers in Alessandro Del Piero and Francesco Totti sacrificed personal attacking ambition for defensive solidarity. I pledged my allegiance to their grit and team spirit.

For the years since, I followed them through good times and bad. In World Cup 2002, I plodded home enraged at the wrongful dismissal of Totti and the incorrectly disallowed goal that helped South Korea knock out Italy. To this day, I maintain that the referee had been paid off. In Euro 2004, denied by the then unknown Zlatan Ibrahimović, Italy's fate came down to the final group stage game. To qualify, they needed to beat Bulgaria *and* the Denmark-Sweden game could not finish 2–2. Antonio Cassano's stoppage-time winner delivered Italy's end of the bargain, but the 2–2 draw at the other game condemned Italy to elimination. Cassano's goal celebration was heartbreaking to watch. He sprinted to the bench to embrace his teammates thinking they had gotten it done, only to be informed of the damning results of the other game. He collapsed in tears, unable to carry on. After the game, Brian and I were two dejected souls wandering the streets of Hong Kong in the wee hours of the morning. In World Cup 2006, after sixteen years of heartbreak and near misses, Italy won their fourth World Cup title. Justin, DJ, Brian, Lulu, and I followed their road to glory across three different time zones, often among hostile opposing fans. My passion for them cooled in 2008; that summer, DJ and I encountered some obnoxious Italian fans during our travels that unsettled my allegiance. In World Cup 2010, a rebuilding Italy crashed out at group stage, a fate that repeated itself four years later in Brazil. With my heroes retiring, I can't name half the players on the team anymore, but some part of me will always be blue.

Tonight, I can finally cheer on the team I have supported my whole life.

After two days of persistent rain, the sky clears up to glorious sunshine. Our train traverses the picturesque countryside.

"Hey, check out the windmills," I point out to Justin.

"Is Holland famous for windmills?" he asks.

"I think so, but I don't know why." I make a mental note to look it up later.

Aside from the occasional banter, the Irish fans leave me more or less in peace.

I fall asleep to the low hum of the train.

I wake up to a tap on my shoulder.

The landscape outside has changed. The country scenery has transitioned to an urban setting. I wonder how long I've slept.

"Hey, check out the pictures from my birthday party," Justin says.

They'd better be so good it was worth waking me up for, I think to myself.

The night before flying to Amsterdam, Justin hosted an early thirtieth birthday party with friends and family at the Hong Kong Club, an exclusive private club whose 1,550 members are admitted by invitation and ballot only. The party's theme was Stephen Chow's character in *From Beijing with Love*, aka "Chinese 007." We must have seen that movie a thousand times growing up. Stephen Chow plays a former spy lured out of retirement for a dinosaur fossil recovery mission. His suitcase is full of useless gadgets—a solar-powered flashlight, an electric shaver disguised as a cell phone, a hair dryer disguised as an electric shaver, yet another hair dryer disguised as a shoe, and a pistol that backfires half the time. In my favorite scene, needing to extract a bullet from a gunshot wound, Stephen Chow hands his partner a VHS tape and asks her to play it on the TV. When a naked woman appears on the screen, he explains that pornography helps channel blood away from the wound and minimize blood loss. Typical guy humor. The movie came out when we were eight. It was funny then, and as our minds grew more corrupt over time, we unlocked new jokes with each rewatch.

I browse through pictures of Justin's party. Everyone looked happy.

"Your dad's suit is pretty badass," I say, referring to Mr. Wong's fierce white Chinese suit. I need one of those to wear to poker games.

Even Lulu and his girlfriend came out of hiding. He seldom hangs out with the boys anymore. Considering he has elected not to come on our trip, I am surprised he has the balls to show up to the party.

"Nice photos. Did you hire a professional?" I ask.

"Yeah. I didn't want the photographer, but somebody paid for it as a gift. It was too much," Justin says.

Yeah right, I think to myself. The photographer was *his* idea.

. . .

The differences between Lille and Amsterdam are striking. Where the Dutch capital embodies contemporary architecture, Lille's buildings are reminiscent of yesteryear. Where Amsterdam's streets are kept clean for the most part, trash and graffiti blemish the roads of Lille. Homelessness is more visible here, if not more prevalent. It's not uncommon to be approached on the subway for money. Commuters fall asleep on their way to work. That Lille's sister city in America is Buffalo, New York says it all.

Our home in Lille is located at a Northern France commune called Villeneuve-d'Ascq.

"The name looks like somebody forgot to finish spelling the word," I comment.

Amandine's apartment will host two Airbnb virgins tonight from Hong Kong. Her place is a fifteen-minute walk from Stade Pierre-Mauroy where the Ireland-Italy clash will take place.

"Are we staying in a house or apartment?" Justin asks.

"No clue."

"Wait, what did you book?"

"I didn't pay attention. I just scrolled through the pictures and picked the best location and price."

Justin looks at me with an incredulous frown.

"Hmm ... I think it's this way," I say, reading the directions on my phone. "But I could be wrong..."

"You serious? Give me your goddamn phone," Justin orders. "We'll be here all day if you navigate."

He finds the housing project in no time. We pause in front of building number fifteen referenced in the instructions.

Justin takes a deep breath. "I guess this is it."

"Should we ring the bell?" I ask.

"Oh ..." Justin stammers, "the door isn't locked ..."

We enter the building and roll our bags through a dark, narrow hallway. We take the elevator to the fifth floor. I ring the apartment bell. A Caucasian girl in her late twenties opens the door. She is skinny and has a white shirt on. She comes across as genuine and easygoing.

"*Bonjour* Amandine!" I cheer in feign excitement.

"Hello Gerald!" she replies, giving me a peck on the cheek.

She gives us a quick tour of her cute three-bedroom home.

"This is your room. Your bed."

Bed ... singular. My heart sinks.

The sofa bed takes up almost the whole room. The only place to sit is on the bed, but there is nothing to lean back on. Two sets of towels are folded on the bed, along with bottles of hotel shower gel and shampoo. The only window is barricaded by steel bars.

"Oh wow, this is great. Thank you so much," I say with a big smile.

"Let me know if you need anything!" she says and leaves the room.

"Yo," Justin mumbles, "does she live here with us or do we have the whole place to ourselves?"

I poke my head outside our room. She is watching TV and folding laundry in the living room. There is an open suitcase on her bedroom floor, but she could be just coming back from a vacation. I can't think of a safe, polite way to ask if she plans to crash at her friend's during our stay.

"Well, she looks pretty settled in, so I'll say no."

We plop down on the flimsy sofa bed.

"My room last weekend at the W Taipei was bigger than this whole apartment," Justin sighs, stretching out on the bed to find a comfortable spot. I move the IKEA canvas print above the headboard so we can at least sit up against the wall. I peek out of the barricaded window, looking for any reason to fall in love with this place.

"Let's go out to eat," I suggest.

We go to lunch at Grand'Place, Lille's central square.

"An Italian fan!" I point. Finally!

"Haha, just one. You're screwed," Justin says.

"I wonder if all the Italian fans are coming on one giant bus and are just stuck somewhere."

Meanwhile, Ireland fans are liquoring up in the plaza. I hope they are not getting ready to fight small fans in blue like me.

We sit down at a French restaurant in the heart of town that has tourist trap written all over it—the outdoor seating, the fancy decor, the pristine linens, and an overzealous hostess.

"You know when I started eating oysters?" Justin says, slurping down half a dozen of *fine de claire.* "Ten years ago when we were in Margarita Island. Remember the guy selling them on the beach?"

Ah, Margarita Island. The magical Margarita Island. How can I ever forget? We stumbled upon this Venezuelan paradise during a four-day layover in Caracas. When DJ hit it off with a group of Colombian girls on the flight, we engineered an itinerary change to move to their resort. From there we lived the four most magical days of our lives. The food and drinks were all-inclusive, as were the beach and sunshine. But our most cherished memories were the time spent with our friends from Colombia. It was innocent, simple, and platonic. Though none of us got any action—a term I am using in the most generous sense—we had the time of our lives. When we bid Margarita Island a tearful goodbye, part of us remained on that island forever. Ten years on, we still look back to those four days drunk on the memory of its perfection.

Our entrées arrive and stir us from our reverie.

"You know who insisted on going to Margarita Island? Lulu. But I don't think we ever gave him any credit for it," I say.

"That bastard," Justin snaps. I have opened a sore subject.

"We have to go back some day. To Margarita Island," I say.

"I have always felt differently," Justin argues. "The second time never lives up to it. Better to just retain that perfect memory."

Justin's seafood entrée is an overcooked piece of white fish on a bed of sauerkraut.

"I hate sauerkraut," he moans.

This puts him in a sour mood for the rest of the meal.

"You know you could have had the three-course special for less."

"Really? Ughh!" he yells, genuinely upset.

"Read the menu, bro."

Piling on is my specialty.

Justin puffs at each bite. This can get out of hand. I better do something.

We settle the bill and search for the only panacea to Justin's woes—Chinese food. We find a dingy hole-in-the-wall place. It's dark and empty. The food behind the counter looks ancient. This isn't a place I would eat at under normal circumstances.

But a hangry Justin is no normal circumstances.

A Chinese man walks out from the kitchen. Without saying a word, he lifts his chin, a universal Chinese gesture that says, "What the hell do you want?"

"Can we have some dumplings?" Justin asks in English.

"*Shen-me?*" the owner grunts.

"*You jiao-zi ma?*" Justin tries again in Mandarin.

With a pair of chopsticks the owner picks up half a dozen dumplings and drop them in the microwave. Sixty seconds later, he serves the steaming dumplings on a paper plate to Justin. I've never seen a chef who looks more unapologetic in serving microwaved food. The dumplings reek of 7-Eleven dim sum, which Justin enjoys on a regular basis. As each dumpling disappears before our eyes, I notice incremental improvement in Justin's morale. Life resembles video games in many ways.

"Happy now?" I ask.

Justin nods and exhales. "How long can you survive without Chinese food?"

"You asked me this already. I don't know."

"What? You've become a *gwei-lo*. I go crazy after a few days. You saw that just now."

Gwei-lo (鬼佬) is Cantonese for "white man."

At Grand'Place, soccer festivities are in full swing. This is every soccer fan's dream. Massive crowds in jerseys are chanting and hoisting their flags. Drinking is done with reckless abandon. Their passion is contagious. Even among Irish fans, I feel welcomed rather than antagonized. We are united by our love for soccer.

"This place is like a massive Nike commercial," Justin says.

I nod.

I wish our friends were here already to share this moment. There are juggling circles as far as the eye can see. In our younger days, we would have dived headfirst into action. When I was a kid, I could juggle for hours on end trying out tricks I saw on TV.

"You know, I still love soccer, but I think my passion has faded," I tell Justin.

"What do you mean? We flew all the way here just to watch soccer!"

"I still follow Man U. But I don't dream about it all day anymore. Soccer and I are like a steady old couple now."

When I moved to California five years ago, the first thing I did was join a soccer team in the San Jose Sunday league. For a long time, that team was my raison d'être. If we lost a game, it would bother me all week. Sometime in the past year, my passion cooled. These days, making it to the final whistle without getting hurt is all I ask for.

We continue our walk around Lille. More soccer fans are out and about as we approach game time.

"Check out those guys."

I point to an odd group of Dutch fans dressed from head to toe in orange. Frolicking in an exceptional spirit that can only be explained by alcohol, they are hoisting a fake European Championship trophy in the air and belting out "*Champione, Champione, olé, olé olé,*" the joke being that the Netherlands didn't even qualify for this tournament.

"At least they have a sense of humor," Justin chuckles.

"You know, every time I see someone in a soccer jersey, I always check the player's name printed on the back," I say.

People's heroes speak volume about them. A "Messi" suggests conformance to mass appeal. The same is true for Real Madrid "Cristiano," though a Manchester United "Cristiano" is held in higher regard. A "Rooney" lives in the past. A "Gerard" is a Liverpool fan. Only a defender wears a defender's jersey. A "Torres" bought the jersey before his inexplicable decline. A "Nasri" places money above loyalty. A "Suárez" signals victory at all cost. A "Nani" points to a life as second fiddle. A "Roy Keane" belongs to an honest, hardworking if troubled man. I have never seen a "Pedro." When I see a "Scholes," I shake your hand. A Manchester United "van Persie" says, "What have you done for me lately?" You don't see a lot of Arsenal "van Persie's" anymore—those were all set ablaze when he defected for Man U. Those who wear "Darren Fletcher," "John O'Shea," "Johnny Evans" or any other lesser-known Manchester United players are my brothers.

Continuing our whirlwind tour of Lille, we survey the Cathédrale Notre-Dame-de -la-Treille on the outside. We see Opéra de Lille and Vieille Bourse in passing. The happenings on the street are far more fascinating. We watch a group of Irish fans (again!) serenade a policewoman. She tries to play it cool, but she looks smitten. Meanwhile, outside Gare de Lille-Flandres, a thousand or so Irish fans are singing folksongs toward a small section of Italian fans. All the smack talk is in good spirit, a stark contrast to the hooligans elsewhere in the tournament. Before the England-Russia game in Marseille, a violent clash broke out between their fans in the old port area. The French police had to disperse the crowd with tear gas.

We head toward the stadium early to beat the crowd. With

two hours till kickoff, fans already have Stade Pierre-Mauroy barricaded. Swimming pools' worth of beer must have been consumed in Lille today.

With music at full blast, the festivities turn up another notch. When some fans notice a window left open on the third floor of a nearby hotel, they take turns trying to kick a soccer ball through from the outside.

"Wow," I say, "the police and hotel staff seem totally cool with it."

We stop for dinner at a restaurant specializing in make-your-own pizza and pasta. Justin piles so many ingredients on his pie that he jams the machine.

"I like my pizza dripping with cheese," he defends.

On TV is the thriller between Hungary and Portugal. Hungary thrice takes the lead but has to settle for a 3–3 draw. With his team's survival hanging by a thread, Ronaldo shows his class. His audacious back heel and towering header propel Portugal into the knockout stage.

We make our slow crawl into the stadium through security.

"Just a pat down and bag search?" I ask, unsure how I feel about it.

I was expecting metal detectors and guards with machine guns. In the US, only see-through bags are allowed in stadiums these days.

"I went to a Beyoncé concert one time. Girls had to throw away their fancy purses outside the stadium," I tell Justin.

"They must really love Beyoncé," Justin says.

Stade Pierre-Mauroy was built in 2012, named in honor of

late former Mayor of Lille and Prime Minister of France Pierre Mauroy. It is home to Lille Olympique Sporting Club and can hold fifty thousand fans at peak. It's a magnificent atmosphere. A grandiose opening ceremony is followed by both national anthems. The energy in the air is electric.

This might as well be a home game for the Irish. Italian fans are outnumbered and lackluster. They look like they don't want to be here but can't resell the tickets.

In our betting group chat, I text Brian, who is in charge of placing all the bets.

All in on Ireland. Halftime draw + Ireland second half win for 6.8x. Trust me.

With qualification already attained, this is a mere run out for the Italian second string. The Irish, in contrast, go home tonight unless they win. Playing with the backing of an entire nation, the boys in green come out like men possessed, ready to fight to the bitter end. Their spirit is contagious. If given a green shirt now, I feel I could take down Cristiano Ronaldo.

You bet yet? Justin texts Brian.

Brian texts back the clenched teeth emoji. I hate when people answer questions with cryptic emojis.

"Brian isn't gonna bet. He doesn't trust us," Justin squawks.

First to every ball and victorious at every fifty-fifty, Ireland dominates from the first whistle. Had they demonstrated more poise in the final third, the game would have been over by halftime. Italian fans are subdued all night aside from when substitute Insigne hits the post.

By the sixtieth minute, Ireland starts to show signs of fatigue. With the clock winding down, a golden chance falls to Ireland.

"That's it! Put it in!" I yell. Sometime over the course of the game, and without realizing myself, I defect.

With just the keeper to beat, Wes Hoolahan somehow scruffs his shot.

"No!!" Justin and I yell, holding our heads in disbelief.

A hum of resignation emerges from the green end of the stadium.

"Man, that was it," I sigh.

But the players aren't giving up yet. In the eighty-fifth minute, Hoolahan receives the ball on the right wing. He takes a touch and sends an in-swinger into the penalty box just beyond the reach of Italian center-back Bonucci. Robbie Brady makes a late run into the box and beats keeper Sirigu for the dramatic game winner.

Italy: 0. Ireland: 1.

"Yeeeaaahhhhhh!!!"

The entire stadium erupts.

Brady knee slides to the corner flag. His teammates pile on in unbridled joy.

"We did it!!! We did it!!!!" Justin and I scream at top of our lungs as the ground vibrates beneath our feet.

All Irish fans are on their feet waving their flag, many of them in tears.

"*Olé, Olé, Olé, Olé!*"

Tonight, everyone is an Irish fan. Tonight, we are all boys in green.

Honks and singing come through our barricaded bedroom window all night.

Tonight, Lille is green.

4

LOVE SONG LITTLE PRINCE — LA CÔTE D'OPALE

I WANT TO BECOME THE JET LI OF MUSIC. –JAY CHOU

"Can you believe we rooted for Ireland last night?" I ask Justin. I wake up this morning feeling like I have cheated on my girlfriend.

"I was neutral all along. You called yourself an Italy fan."

We rock, paper, scissor to see who has to get up first. Justin loses.

He stumbles out of the room. I hear a swift opening and closing of the bathroom door.

"Ah! sorry," Justin gasps as he backs out of the bathroom.

Still half asleep and in his boxers, he barges in and ambushes Amandine brushing her teeth.

"Ughh ... I hate living with other people," he complains.

"Good. You better get rich then," I yawn.

Since we've already seen most of Lille yesterday, we decide to rent a car and check out the coast today. After yesterday's madness, peace is restored in Lille. Many Ireland fans are passed out on benches, looking the worse for wear. But hangover and self-hatred are short-lived; memories of last night will last a lifetime.

Car rental companies are my mortal enemies. Their policies are designed for maximum customer inconvenience. In my most gregarious self, I force a smile and approach the lady at the Europcar counter.

"Pass-a-por, please," she says.

"Excuse me?" I reply. I don't have my passport with me.

"Pass-a-por, please," she repeats.

"There's a picture on my driver's license. Would that work?" I ask.

"*Non*. In all rental companies you need driver's license, pass-a-por, and an international driver's license. Driver's license, pass-a-por, and international driver's license," she repeats slowly. "At Europcar we are cool and don't need an international driver's license. But you need driver's license and pass-a-por."

Europcar may be many things—clean, affordable, accessible ... But they sure aren't cool.

I also know that car rental companies never bend their rules. So back to *Chez Amandine* we go for pass-a-por.

A torrential downpour breaks out just as we emerge from the subway station at Villeneuve-d'Ascq. It is as if God is mocking me for my rookie car rental mistake.

"Just wait for me in the mall," I tell Justin.

There is no reason he should have to get wet. Let a man pay for his own mistake.

When I return to the mall, I am drenched and still fuming at my own stupidity. I leave a water trail on the white tile floor in my wake, much to the displeasure of the mall janitor. My day is off to an awful start.

I find Justin on a bench. He has a mischievous look on his face.

"Look what I got us for breakfast," Justin says, his lips curl to a smile.

From a plastic bag he unveils a bento box—salmon sashimi on rice. In the center, a tiny yellow chrysanthemum sprouts from a dab of wasabi. I rip open the plastic packages of soy sauce and spread it all over the rice.

"Only you would do something like this," I chuckle.

In a deserted mall, we pass the sashimi bowl back and forth on an otherwise miserable morning. Leave it to Justin to cheer you up.

"Hi again," I say, waving my pass-a-por as we return to Europcar.

Moments later we leave the Europcar office with car keys jingling in my pocket. A gray Clio awaits.

"Wow, sweet ride. Check out this door," Justin yells.

From his reaction, I was expecting swing-up doors like a Lamborghini. It turns out Justin has never seen a rear door handle installed on the window, a low-cost feature if anything. Justin doesn't own his own car. When he needs to go somewhere, he chooses from his family garage—Tesla Model S and a roster of Mercedes that seems to change every season. He is so accustomed to luxury cars that he finds cheap European cars exotic.

"What's wrong with you? *Fu-yee-doy*," I say. *Fu-yee-doy* (富二代), which translates to "rich second generation," is a new term that mocks the children of rich families.

But at least this cheap European car is brand-new and clean. It comes with a USB port, Bluetooth, and even built-in navigation. Justin needs no invitation to put on his Cantonese playlist. We buckle up and fiddle with the mechanical latches to adjust our seats.

"Ready?" I look to Justin, testing out the loose clutch and turning the ignition. With the stereo turned all the way up, we escape a city engulfed by dark clouds into the blue-skied country.

"Remember our Mustang in LA?" I ask. "Today would be a good day for it."

Three years ago Justin and I did a road trip in Los Angeles. I had just broken up with my longtime girlfriend. In our rental Mustang convertible, we drove along the Pacific Coast as he unpeeled the onion that was my five-year relationship. It was sweatshirt weather in Southern California. The leaves were starting to turn. We posed for pictures under the Hollywood sign. We visit the Universal Studios on fast passes. We lay in bed in our hotel room and listened to Chinese music.

"I've been there, bro," he said during our long stroll along Santa Monica beach. "It took me years to get over my last girlfriend."

We walked out to the pier in silence. Against the beautiful ocean backdrop, he snapped a series of selfies and shared them with his love interest at the time.

"Check this out. I am a pro at editing photos now."

He took a candid photo of me and hunched over his phone for minutes. He then showed me the end product that looked album cover worthy.

I forced a chuckle. "Why is my face all orange?"

We flexed our muscles for a picture at the Muscle Beach gym at Venice Beach.

"When we get back to the room, I'll play you some Jay Chou."

I smiled.

"You know what they call me?" he asked. "情歌小王子. 'Love Song Little Prince.'"

I laughed.

"Hey, I've an idea. Let's take off our shirts and reenact this photo," he said.

He showed me a picture we took years ago on Margarita Island. In our Quicksilver board shorts, we spread our arms for the camera as if embracing the universe. We didn't have a care in the world.

Justin knows how to cheer people up. He is romantic to a fault. I can understand why all his ex-girlfriends have a hard time saying goodbye.

After our Venice Beach photoshoot, we went back to the hotel. He set his iPad on the table and plugged in the speakers.

"Stand here and listen," he instructed. "Pay really close attention to the lyrics."

I listened to the first verse of Jay Chou's 哪裡都是妳, which means "You Are Everywhere."

"This is a good one for you right after a breakup ... Oh, this other one is even better, 明明就, especially after she scored a new boyfriend."

That was three years ago. Here we are now on another road trip. But this time, instead of nursing my love wounds, I am trying to decide when to propose to Molly.

"Has she hinted she wants to get married?" Justin asks.

I nod.

It was more than a hint. In fact, last Christmas when she brought it up, we agreed to be engaged by the following July. I am not opposed to the idea, but if we are happy now, why change?

It's July next month.

"Well, we'll have plenty of time the next few weeks to talk about it," Justin says.

I go to Justin for relationship advice because he's far more experienced. Girls love him. During our teenage years, we used to go out a lot every Christmas and summer break. Before eighteen, we frequented the only bar in Lan Kwai Fong that served minors. Everyone our age was there, and every night we met up with friends and got introduced to their other friends. When girls met Justin in person for the first time, I could always tell which ones already knew of him but were trying to play it cool. He was good-looking and well connected. We once even found a fake Facebook account someone had created using photos harvested from Justin's accounts. To this day we still haven't figured out what happened.

I've met all Justin's past girlfriends, but we've never made it past "hi-bye." Sometimes, I wonder if they even remember my name. I try to keep my distance from my friends' girlfriends; this way I don't lose a friend when they break up. Also, if they ever get in a fight, I want to be on the guy's side even when he is in the wrong. It is easier to do that if I don't know her well.

I was introduced to Justin's current girlfriend, Vincy, at a karaoke six months ago. She was throwing a going-away party for her best friend and Justin invited me to join. Arriving late, I barged into a roomful of strangers. There was a massive drinking game going, but Justin was all by himself sitting in the corner.

"Why aren't you playing?" I asked.

"I'm freaking out about asking her to be my girlfriend," he mumbled.

They had been seeing each other for two months. He was slow-playing this hand, but not because he had pocket aces. He thought she was out of his league.

"I don't want to screw this one up," Justin explained.

I did a double take. Take it slow? Justin Wong? He was a man of theatrics and was always ahead of his time. "Taking it slow" must be the new black.

He ordered a six-pack to share.

"Let's drink some beer and catch up. Glad to see you, bro."

Over Budweiser he told me everything about Vincy. He told me about their perfect first date, how he'd lined up a backup plan should conversation dry up, and how the past two months had been "different."

"She checked every box," he said, "even ones I didn't previously know existed."

"Should I say hi?" I asked.

"Sure," he said. He wanted my opinion, and maybe felt I would put in a good word. I went over to talk to her.

From the start, Vincy treated me like a good friend, and seemed to take a genuine interest in what I had to say. Everything Justin had raved about her held true. In the noisy karaoke room, we carved out an island of peace for a candid heart-to-heart. She asked me about "the real Justin."

"Well," I chuckled, staring into the velvet red walls to buy time. The room descended into an eerie silence as I searched for something safe to say. I wished she had asked me before the Budweiser.

"Justin has his ups and downs—biiiig ups and biiiig downs.

But if you can get through all that," I paused before continuing, "deep down he's not a bad guy."

It was the truth. He was a great friend; how he was as a boyfriend was something she had to find out herself.

She laughed. "Oh it's okay. I have mood swings, too."

I smiled, wondering how much of Justin she had seen so far.

"Is he scared of me?" She switched topics.

"Don't worry about it," I said, shaking my head. "He's trying to take it slow."

The next day, Justin invited me to the country club pool, where I spent three hours in his company listening to more Vincy talk. That night, Justin and Vincy ran into his brother Jasper at a club, where he introduced Vincy as his future wife. So he took it slow in asking her to be his girlfriend, but went full speed in introducing her as his wife.

All this without even holding hands yet.

Hats off to you, Master Wong.

And now, they are six months along in a happy relationship. Driving down the French countryside and hearing Justin gush about her, I can tell he is smitten with this girl.

"So you guys held hands yet?" I ask.

"Hmm...*ying-goi* went beyond that."

Ying-goi (應該) is Cantonese for "probably." Like *bay-gao* ("relatively"), Justin and I use it sarcastically.

"So what's in Dunkirk?" Justin asks.

I want to visit Dunkirk for three reasons. One, it's on the way to the beautiful Cap Blanc-Nez. Two, it played a historic role during WWII. Three, Samuel Eells.

Who is Samuel Eells?

He was born in 1810 in Westmoreland, New York. An intellectual powerhouse and a man of immense character, Eells battled health issues all his life. One day, he took to sailing to bolster his health. In an ultimate irony, he got sicker during the trip, succumbing to a case of cholera so severe that the crew abandoned him at Dunkirk. Left to die on a dock, Eells convinced two little boys to get him calomel and hot water. Through sheer will, he rallied back to life and went on to found the Alpha Delta Phi fraternity.

"Why are you telling me this story?" Justin asks.

"Because Alpha Delta Phi was my fraternity in college," I explain. I owe every ounce of my beer pong skill to this man. I hope to find that famous dock in Dunkirk where it all began.

We arrive at Dunkirk not knowing what to see. I'd asked my mom to do some research.

Checked Dunkirk and Calais. Not much to do. Maybe war museums. Go to the beach, she wrote back with links to a few articles, which I didn't click into.

"Let's ask the locals," I suggest to Justin.

A warm, middle-aged lady at the tourism office gets up from her desk to greet us.

"Welcome to Dunkirk," she says. Her handshake is warm.

We ask her what there is to do around here.

"*Oh là là*," she exclaims, taken aback by the banana prints on Justin's Donkey Kong T-shirt. "You have to visit our Harbor Museum. They have lots of bananas there."

"Oh yeah, Justin loves bananas," I giggle.

We promise to stop by; we need a photo of Justin and the bananas.

"Also, Christopher Nolan is shooting a movie here now. It's called *Dunkirk*," she adds.

The movie, coming to theaters in 2017, is based on the historic WWII evacuation that took place in this very town. Surprise, surprise.

"What about Calais?" I ask.

"Oh, there's not much to see," she says.

Perhaps she wants to dissuade interest from the Walking-Dead-like event last week. Three hundred migrants charged the port of Calais in an attempt to smuggle onto UK-bound ferries. Bricks were thrown in audacious carjack attempts. Police resorted to teargas to disperse the crowd. In the migrant encampment known as "Calais Jungle," six thousand refugees are waiting for an opening to illegally enter the UK. Most are refugees from Sudan, Afghanistan and Syria, running away from the violence of their home countries in search of a better life. It is tragic.

We walk to the Musée Portuaire to make good on our promise.

"I wonder why she wouldn't stop raving about these bananas," I say.

According to the "*Extra Ordinaire Banane*" exhibition here, Dunkirk was the first French port that imported bananas. Today, Del Monte ships forty thousand tons of bananas a year from Cameroon into Europe via Dunkirk. Standing here in a fortress of banana crates, I sense this is where Eells stared death in the face and said, "Thanks, but no thanks." It has to be.

Our next stop is Musée Dunkerque 1940—the War Museum.

"This used to be an actual fortification built in 1874 to reinforce France's coastal defense," Justin reads from the sign.

The museum weaves the incredible story of the Evacuation of Dunkirk. We pay our respect to the lost Allied soldiers, without whose gallantry our world would look very different.

We find a place along the beach for lunch. There is one thing we've come here to eat—*moules marinière*. The restaurant serves mussels in two styles: white-wine-based and tomato-based.

"Both please," Justin says.

Our waiter lets out a nervous laugh.

"No, no. Just the white wine please," I clarify.

Sampling regional French cuisine, enchanted by the stunning ocean view and humbled by this place's historical significance, we decide to talk, of all things, politics.

"So you think Trump will win?" Justin switches topic while maintaining full eye contact with his mussels.

"Really don't know man," I reply, doing the same. "Maybe."

"Time to move back to Hong Kong, right?"

I chuckle.

He asks me that question a lot, and I always give the same answer.

After college, I spent three years in Upstate New York. During that time, I thought about moving back to Hong Kong all the time. Things changed when I moved to San Francisco in 2012. My new job requires traveling to Asia several times a year. Flying through Hong Kong allows me to see my family and friends, even just for a short stay. I am quite happy with my life now.

Justin and I don't see eye to eye on this. He's a traditional man who believes that coming home is man's ultimate destiny, a "when" question, not "if." After college in the UK, he sealed his return and never looked back. When he was applying for his MBA, his search extended to the US, but in the end the idea of two years away from Hong Kong didn't appeal to him.

"I don't think I can ever leave Hong Kong for good," he often tells me.

I can relate to that. Hong Kong is an exciting, glamorous city. We have amazing restaurants serving cuisines from all over the world, from hole-in-the-wall places to Michelin-starred establishments. Though we will never qualify for the World Cup in my lifetime, Hong Kong's passion for soccer is undeniable, even before sports gambling. Our public transportation is the envy of any metropolitan city. Our subway is clean, easy, and reliable. It can be a complex city to navigate with all the gossips and backstabs, but we grew up there and know our way around, literally and figuratively. Most importantly, our friends and family are there.

After college, I too considered moving back to Hong Kong. The sentimental side of me wanted to. The pragmatic side reasoned that for an engineer, the US afforded more opportunities. In the end, the pragmatic side pays the bills. My family was supportive of the idea, even though it meant seeing me only once a year. They too were practical people. In the eight years since, not one day goes by that I don't think about Hong Kong, every January, especially when I fly back to the States after the holidays. Nostalgia used to torment me, but I'm used to it now. Maybe Justin is right; I have become a *gwei-lo*.

After lunch, we saunter along the very beach where three

hundred and thirty-eight thousand Allied soldiers evacuated during WWII. Today, a marble memorial stands in Dunkirk, with the following inscribed in French: *To the glorious memory of the pilots, mariners, and soldiers of the French and Allied armies who sacrificed themselves in the Battle of Dunkirk, May – June 1940.*

The movie *Atonement* depicted Dunkirk beach as a fallen paradise. In the delirium of complete despair, stranded Allied soldiers drank to abandon. Horses ran wild. Buildings were burned to rubble against the backdrop of an abandoned Ferris wheel. Today, there is little evidence of WWII sorrow. Charming houses add a riot of colors to the beach. Remnants of the war have long been washed away.

"What's in Le Cap Blanc-Nez?" Justin asks as we drive along the ocean toward the next destination.

"It's the highest point along the Opal Coast. Spectacular view apparently."

We park our car and hike up to the edge of the land. Standing at the cliff under the overcast sky, we behold the vast English Channel beneath us. With good eyes, you can make out the silhouette of England from the distance.

"After this trip, I'm taking Vincy on a road trip. I will drive to Dover and look back from the other side," Justin says.

"You ever considered writing romance novels?"

When it comes to love, Justin spares no expenses. His Valentine's Day dinners are the stuff of legends. He prepares a ten-course meal that takes weeks just to source the ingredients. He also schedules a dry run a week before and leaves nothing to chances. He sets a bad example for all men.

"What's that?" Justin asks, pointing at an obelisk atop the cape.

"It's to honor the Dover Patrol. They protected this Franco-British channel from the Germans during WWI." I strain my eyes to read the fine print engraved on the monument. "I miss Lulu."

When we visited new places, Lulu always had his guidebooks and would read aloud word for word like a tour guide. It was the same Lulu who decided not to come on this trip.

"Screw Lulu," Justin says.

"Yo! Are you done? Enough already!" I yell.

We've been standing on this spot for almost thirty minutes taking pictures.

"Did I ever tell you why I was so upset about losing my phone?" Justin asks.

He lost his phone a few weeks ago after a night out. He was unreachable for days and I was beginning to wonder if he was going to pull a "Lulu" on me.

"'Coz you lost all your pictures?"

He shakes his head.

"One day, I downloaded a movie editing software on my phone and taught myself how to use it. You know how bad I am with technology right?"

I nod.

"I took all our footgolf videos from Vegas and condensed them into a one-minute clip. I spent like three hours one Saturday doing that. I was gonna give you that for your birthday."

For my thirtieth birthday, Justin and Kenny planned a

surprise birthday trip for me in Las Vegas. We ate, drank, partied, and gambled. We also played a round of footgolf at the Siena Golf Club. Justin took a lot of videos during our round. It didn't occur to me then that he was trying to make a video for me. I can picture Justin in his living room, tearing his hair out trying to figure out the video editing app.

I stare out to the ocean. Justin continues to take photos of Le Cap Blanc-Nez in silence. They say that the best thing about memories is making them.

"There's a footgolf place not too far from here in Arras," I say. "Loser pays for dinner?"

Footgolf is the brainchild of ex-Barcelona player Juan Manuel Asensi. It's a game of golf played with a soccer ball and your feet. Since its induction in the 2000s, it has gathered some serious momentum around the world.

"I hate to break it to you," I say as we pull into Golf d'Arras, a heavy sky hanging ominously overhead, "but your head is gonna get a little wet today."

The drizzle breaks into a full-fledged downpour. The river that snakes through the course has overflown its trough. Because footgolf is played on actual golf courses but with shortened yardage and modified hole sequence, signage is often makeshift and unclear. By the third hole, we're both ready to quit. Half of footgolf is navigation, which is made much more difficult by the rain and soggy terrain. Justin is usually the better player, but his game doesn't fare well in the rain. He'll be buying dinner tonight.

We head back to Lille after a sumptuous three-course

dinner in downtown Arras. When we stop for gas, Justin buys a cup of chicken soup from the vending machine.

"Check this out. Isn't this cool?" he says.

"Didn't we just eat dinner? How does it taste?"

"Hmm ... average. Too powdery. See?"

He shows me the residual powder at the bottom of the cup.

"Get some hot water and you can have a second serving."

We are spent by the time we get home, but I have to say hi to Ramïn, Amandine's husband. They are in the midst of an origami project at the kitchen table.

"What are these for?" I ask.

"Our wedding. We marry mid-July," Ramïn replies.

In my mind, I weave the backstory of this young couple. Ramïn and Amandine hunched over the dim kitchen lamp every night folding paper cranes. They whisper in each other's ears, wary of waking up their Airbnb guests behind thin walls. The inconvenience of sharing their love nest with strangers is made bearable by the possibilities this extra income will bring —a life with each other.

"You guys left really early this morning," Ramïn says, interrupting my thoughts. "We had breakfast made for you but you didn't eat."

My imaginary turntable screeches to a halt.

Let me rewrite their backstory: When Ramïn came home from work and found our breakfast went untouched, he threw the plate against the wall and yelled at Amandine. She was quick to come to our defense, but he didn't listen. He plopped into a wooden chair and started folding paper cranes, spewing hate through gritted teeth.

There was never any mention of breakfast, I want to tell

him, but perhaps it was implied through Airbn*b*? Wanting to part on amicable terms, I apologize and ask him not to worry about making breakfast tomorrow. I never turn down a free lunch (or breakfast), but like Justin said, staying here feels like being taken in as a favor.

When I get back to our room, Justin is in bed on his phone, already showered.

"Amandine looks prettier today," he mumbles before drifting off to sleep.

I wake up the next morning to hundreds of texts. These days, we've become slaves to our devices. Unread emails give me anxiety. Sometimes, even personal messages can feel over-whelming.

The WhatsApp discussion du jour is the "Brexit" vote. By the time we step out into Amandine's living room, we are well briefed on the latest.

"Emm ... the UK is ... em ... leaving Euro," Amandine announces, fumbling for the right English words.

I nod. "Yeah, we heard."

"I am so ... so ... shocked," she stammers.

In spite of the EU's existential crisis, our journey resumes. Justin and I bid Amandine a cheerful goodbye and board a Ouibus to Paris. How Ouibus stays in business charging us five euros each is beyond me.

"When's Brian arriving?" I ask. Justin has his headphones on and is about to fall asleep.

"Tomorrow morning. Probably so he doesn't have to pay for the hotel tonight. That CB (cheap bastard)."

GOYARD YOURSELF — PARIS

WHEN WE GET off the bus at Paris's La Défense, I insist on walking to our hotel.

The route looks innocuous enough on Apple Maps. It doesn't occur to me that we will have to traverse a network of interlocking highways and overhead walkways.

"It's like finding your way in a city in the sky," I say, trying to catch my breath.

We haven't eaten yet, and the urgency in Justin's footsteps is reminiscent of Lille before the microwave dumplings.

"Maybe we should have taken Ramïn up on the breakfast," I say.

"Where's this place?" Justin roars, getting impatient.

We circle the block for what feels like hours, negotiating up and down flights of stairs as our water supply dwindles. When the hotel entrance appears behind some man-made trees, we feel as if we have discovered The Lost City of Z.

"*Bonjour!*" the hotel receptionist gives us a war hero's welcome. "It must have been a long journey."

Her name is Isabelle. She is the girl-next-door of every

guy's dream. Blue eyes, wavy brown hair in a ponytail, and a melodious voice that erases our woes. I allow myself to picture growing up with her in the meadows, me herding sheep and her strumming the guitar writing country tunes. One day, we move to the city to chase her music dream. In a *petit* Paris apartment, we raise two kids—Hugo and Mathilde —along with Coco, a cocker spaniel.

"Enjoy your stay." She hands over our room keys. We miss her already.

After two nights with Amandine, we return to a proper hotel room.

"Wow, two bedrooms! Nice!" I cheer. I would have settled for just my own bed!

"This place isn't luxurious by any stretch, but shit it's nice to shower not having to worry about knocking over Amandine's jewelry," Justin says.

After Paris, we will stay in Airbnbs in Lyon, Monaco, Saint-Tropez, and Marseille. We will have an apartment in Barcelona and a villa in Ibiza, but by then the whole crew will have arrived. Living conditions will only deteriorate from here on out.

Let's enjoy our own bed while we can tonight.

Famished, we charge our phones and head over to the metro station. When we see a departing train with food advertisements all over, we hop on without thinking. Primal instincts.

"Oops, wrong direction," I realize once the doors close.

"*Hui been ah?*" an Asian lady asks in Cantonese.

We do a double take.

I tell her we are looking for food. Speaking Cantonese to a stranger in Paris feels both awkward and comforting.

She tells us about the big mall at the next stop. And we should check out the sale while there. Shopping is the last thing on our minds now, but we thank her all the same.

"Nice lady," Justin says.

She sits down next to her half-Caucasian daughter and talks to her in fluent French.

"She reminds me of my Goo-ma in New Jersey, whom you're going to meet in Ibiza," I tell Justin.

In English, all relatives are uncles, aunts and cousins. Chinese salutations are more specific. Goo-ma is the elder sister of my dad. She left Hong Kong for the US as a teenager. After forty years in the States, she still speaks good Cantonese and disapproves of the new slang Hong Kong teenagers use these days. When I look at her, I see myself in thirty years. Try as I might to keep pace with Hong Kong's latest culture, I've had hillbilly moments of my own. One time when we were entering a beach party, the bouncer handed me a plastic cup.

"What's this for?" I asked my friends. I was holding a glass bottle of Corona and should have connected the dots.

Justin gave me a weird look. "Umm ... what do you think? *Ying-goi* (應該) not for donating sperm."

After lunch, we stroll down Champs-Élysées. Anthony Bourdain once said that nothing unexpected or wonderful is likely to happen if you have an itinerary in Paris filled with the Louvre and the Eiffel Tower.

"Let's save those for when we come back with our wives," Justin says.

I nod. A leisurely route around Paris sounds good to me.

We emerge from the metro station to the glorious sight of

the Arc de Triomphe. Leisurely route or not, a selfie is in order.

"Look at this guy." I point out a young Caucasian man in an ornate flower hat.

He has the same idea as us, but on a whole different level. Balancing a full-sized SLR camera in one hand, a flash in another and rocking some serious Blue Steel, he takes a candid selfie before the Arc de Triomphe. My own vanity pales in comparison.

What people would do these days to get a good shot.

More texts from my mom. Ever since I offered her tickets to the Quarter-Final, she has taken a sudden interest in the tournament.

What are the likely teams we will see in Semi-Final in Marseille? she asks.

Quarter-Final. Croatia and Switzerland. Not good. I reply.

Why not good? she asks.

Could have been Spain and Germany, I write.

Oh. No wonder. Still exciting for me.

With the European Championship in full swing, soccer ads are out in full force. For a Man U fan, seeing the Paul Pogba billboards all over Paris is like finding an ex-girlfriend on the cover of *Sports Illustrated*. Frustrated by the lack of first team opportunity, the nineteen-year-old French boy left Manchester United for Juventus in 2012. He has been tearing it up in *Serie A* since, winning four straight league titles. Meanwhile, his old team, which received a petty eight hundred thousand pounds from Juventus in the transfer, has been languishing since the retirement of our longtime manager Sir Alex Ferguson. We can use a

Pogba now. Our new coach Mourinho is rumored to spend one hundred million pounds to bring home the prodigal son, probably to the tune of Katy Perry's *The One That Got Away*.

Justin and I laze on the chaise longues at the Jardin des Tuileries. We lean back, sedated under the vastness of the baby blue sky. This is *chillaxing à la Parisienne*.

"We can get a twelve-pack of Bud Light and sit here all afternoon," Justin says.

"Dude ..." I mumble with my eyes closed. "Of all the beers in the world, you fantasize about Bud Light."

We sit in peace for minutes. I might even have fallen asleep.

"Have you heard of Goya?" Justin asks out of the blue.

"Like the canned beans?"

"No, a luxury brand supposedly. Oh, Goyard, not Goya."

"Nope."

"My girlfriend wants me to get this for her," he says, showing me a picture on his phone.

I open one eye to look.

"Oh, a tote bag," I say.

"Yeah. How do you know what a tote bag is?"

I sit back up. "You of all people don't know?"

Justin has a closet that would put some European royalty to shame. He would never be caught dead with the wrong outfit for any social occasion. Outside of sports and school uniforms, I can't recall him ever repeating an outfit.

The Goyard store is just two blocks from the Tuileries. A doorman guards the storefront with a tally counter to control traffic. There are only a handful of customers inside, but he still makes us wait.

"This is just like Levels," Justin scoffs, referring to a dance club in Hong Kong notorious for keeping a long line out front to generate fake hype.

Unfortunately for Goyard, waiting in a fake line is not generally how I like to begin spending thousands of dollars.

When our turn comes, Justin strides straight to the counter and brings up the tote bag picture.

The store attendant sizes us up.

"Wait a minute please," he says.

In white gloves, he produces an antique key from his pocket, which he uses to unlock the merchandise cabinet. Gently, he lays the bag down on the counter and removes a piece of lint. Justin takes a picture on his phone.

"No photo please," the attendant mutters.

Justin texts Vincy the price.

"*€ 1,040? Omg so cheaappp,*" Vincy replies.

A 1,040-euro beach bag to hold your towel, Nicholas Sparks novel, and SPF 50 Banana Boat.

"Ok, I'll take it," Justin says.

He pulls out his phone again, turns to me, and says, "Yell at me now for taking photos. I dare you."

I laugh.

"I did a case study on LVMH for school. The professor said that buying luxury goods is about the overall experience. I'm going to milk the shit out of the experience."

We walk to the cashier to pay. Our attendant has Vincy's tote wrapped up in a maroon gift bag, but won't hand it over until the credit card clears.

"This feels more like hostage exchange," I say.

Our Goyard experience sparks a lengthy discussion for the

rest of the afternoon—what is the most expensive thing we've ever bought?

"Exclude cell phones, computers, and other practical items," I clarify.

"Alcohol," Justin says right away. "No contest."

Most of his damage is self-inflicted. He earned his nickname "Mr. Dom Pérignon" from the regrettable financial decisions made under the delirium of alcohol. Drinking lowers his inhibition and leads to more money spent on alcohol. A deadly downward spiral.

But it hasn't always been his fault. Once at a club he was approached by a girl who was one hundred percent his type—long hair, fair skin, and a quiet mystique. She was a black-belt seductress who sprinkled Justin with just enough attention between long stretches of aloofness. Justin was defenseless against that kind of gameplay, and when she hinted she wanted to drink Dom Pérignon, he didn't think twice. Later, he found out that she was a Dom Pérignon promoter at the club.

"I learned a four-thousand-Hong-Kong-dollar lesson that night," he says.

Other times, it was being in the wrong place at the wrong time. A couple years ago, he went out with people he didn't know well. He stayed till the end and when it came time to pay, everyone vanished. He ended up footing a giant bill.

"I was depressed for a very long time," he says.

His generosity is also to blame for many financial pitfalls. When we were in Los Angeles a few years ago, he brought his cousin and me to a high-end Japanese restaurant and introduced us to *omakase*, an expensive Japanese meal that translates to "chef's selection." Each dish was prepared fresh before us and served with specific eating instructions. The majesty of Japanese cuisine was on full display. I learned that some sushi you shouldn't eat with wasabi and soy sauce.

"Hey, anything you guys want to repeat?" Justin asked at the end of the meal.

"Repeat?"

"Don't worry. It's free. When you go to *omakase*, they feed you till you're full. I repeat all the time in Hong Kong," he said, unapologetic about asking for more food.

His cousin and I studied the menu again, still skeptical.

"Don't be shy guys. When you do *omakase*, you need a big stomach and thick skin. If you're too shy to ask, Captain will do it for you," he said, pounding his chest.

Under Captain's order, we repeated uni, toro, and half a dozen of nigiris. When the bill came, Justin couldn't believe his eyes.

"Ehh...I guess they don't do free repeats here in LA," Captain conceded.

The answer is clear—food and drinks make Justin poor.

"What else?" I ask.

We've settled down at a café in the eleventh arrondissement for an early cocktail. We have no clue how we've ended up here.

Justin thinks for a moment. "Maybe gambling."

He loves roulette, which offers one of the worst expected returns outside of slot machines. He isn't shy to spend his winnings either. One time, after making HK$4,000 betting on Real Madrid, he drove straight to the Prada outlet in Hong Kong.

"Do you still go to casinos a lot?" Justin asks.

"Yup," I nod. "Blackjack mostly. But I've gotten into fantasy sports in recent years, too."

I love gambling. The thrill is intoxicating. Nothing brings greater joy than watching the blackjack dealer turn over a bust card. I love blackjack even knowing the house wins all the time. I visit Las Vegas every Easter.

"What's fantasy football?" Justin asks.

"Basically you build a team by drafting different players across the league. You accumulate points based on the player's actual performance and every week you go up against an opponent."

We don't play for big money, but during football season, I spend hours a day smack talking and doing players research. I'm addicted.

"What about your biggest expenses?" Justin asks.

Air travel. Without a doubt.

My father likes to shame me for my high carbon footprint. I fly to Asia at least twice a year to see my friends, sometimes through work, sometimes pure leisure.

It all began five years ago on a trip to Taipei. It was spring of 2011. We were at the midway point of our twenties, where a boys' trip out of the country was still a distant dream. Only a few years removed from college, we were starting at the bottom of the totem pole where pay was meager and hours long. Brian, Justin, and Lulu were laboring away in Hong Kong's infamous accounting industry. Brian once spent twenty-one days straight working out of a hotel room in Macau; Justin traveled to Inner Mongolia to count windmills (final count was twenty-five). Those who earned their accounting stripes in Hong Kong would sympathize with their plight. Victim to a slow job market post-2008, DJ took a job as a lowly compliance analyst, a job he accepted without a clue of what compliance was.

"Looking back, I think that job suited me well," DJ once told me. "I learned that rules are meant to be broken. It's whether or not you get caught doing so. In the end, I decided to play the good guy and catch those assholes."

Things weren't any easier for me. In the spring semester of my senior year, I landed an engineering job at a concrete construction company in New Jersey. It wasn't my dream job, but in a tough job market, I was grateful for anything. The start date wasn't until July, which would give me all of spring semester and the month of June to cruise before adult life began in earnest. Like my fellow college seniors, I did just that.

A week before Commencement, I received a call from my future manager.

"Hey," he began in a somber tone, "we are laying off a lot of people because of the economy."

I was outside barbecuing with my friends; I wondered if he could hear the rap music and the *thump* of cornhole in the background.

He said they could no longer hire me.

I told him I understood.

"You're taking this very well," he said.

"Thank you."

The call lasted two minutes. We went our separate ways and never heard from each other again.

"Who was that?" my then girlfriend asked.

I took a swig of Miller Lite.

"I think I just got laid off," I replied.

The magnitude of the news didn't hit me until long after we had hung up. The company offered a small severance compensation, which funded my trip to Europe with DJ that summer.

When we returned from Europe, I went back to the metaphorical drawing board. I was staying at my Goo-ma's when I got a call from a company I didn't recall applying to. They had an opening for water-processing engineer and asked if I was still interested.

"Yes, yes!" I said, sounding more desperate than I wanted.

I read up on their company right away. I also dusted off my fluid dynamics textbook, a class I was lucky to escape with a B.

I made two long trips from my aunt's house in New Jersey to Upstate New York for interviews, taking the dreadful four-hour bus ride I used to hate during my college days. On the bus, I racked my brains for reasons why this company would hire me. Deep down I knew I had immense character, but on paper I was a cookie-cutter college grad. My grades were average. The only "internship" on my résumé was as a park volunteer in Costa Rica, which I quit after a week. I feared my lack of practical experience would expose my secret lack of interest in Engineering. I knew Mechanical Engineering wasn't for me halfway through my sophomore year. Some people get excited about pulleys, robots, and machine shops. And then there are people like me. The inner workings of the world didn't interest me, and I didn't want to get my hands dirty. I read books under the desk during all my Engineering lectures—Fitzgerald, Hemingway, Golding, Murakami, McCourt, Vonnegut, and other classics borrowed from the university library. I spent free periods in the library stacks looking for my next read. I didn't understand most of them, but I found them enjoyable nonetheless. I had always thought of myself as a science person; I was beginning to question if I had gotten it wrong all along.

Not knowing my true passion, I stuck with Mechanical Engineering on the belief that a technical degree would leave many doors open. During my job search, I applied to everything else—journalism, consulting, retail, and even fashion. None of those worked out. Being an engineer was my fallback plan, and here I was making the trip to Cortland to cash in on my safety net.

At the interview, they didn't ask any technical questions, which was a relief. Instead, they wanted examples of conflict management. I leaned on experiences from various soccer teams I had played on. There was nothing spectacular about my answers, and I couldn't get a good read from my interviewers' expressions.

"What would you do here in your free time?" a senior engineer asked during the final panel interview.

He seemed skeptical that I would settle in the area. Hong Kong to Cortland, New York, was a big leap.

"Well, I like soccer. I like golf. I like to write. I would get to do those things here," I told them the truth, but I didn't think they believed me. "I still have friends at Cornell, but I don't want to be *that* guy who hangs around campus forever."

They laughed.

I didn't know what they saw. In the end, they took a chance on me. To this day, I am grateful for that. While most of my classmates were moving to Los Angeles, Manhattan, Boston, and Washington, D.C., I packed up for Cortland.

"You're crazy," they all said.

"At least I have a job," I said.

Besides, Cornell was only thirty minutes away so I could continue to see my then girlfriend.

I spent three years working with some great, dignified people who taught me everything from pump curves and electrical drawings to American football and retirement accounts. In the beginning, there were moments of culture shock. One day, I brought bags of bottles to the local recycling center. When the machine rejected bottles of certain dimensions, I found the nearest dumpster and threw them away. Just as I was walking back to my car, a stocky fellow in a trucker hat came up to me, clearly upset about something.

"Take your trash out of my dumpster now or I'll call the police."

Lesson learned—don't mess with people's trash cans.

It didn't take me long to settle in. In the winter, which could last upward of eight months, karate classes at the local YMCA kept me fit. Movies and homemade chicken soup became my weekend ritual. I started swimming again and even drove hours across states to compete. The luscious summers in Upstate are short but beautiful. On Thursday nights, I teamed up with a good group of guys in a golf league. Larry and his son owned a cleaning business. Tim played in college and was trying to be a state trooper. They were fun and down-to-earth people who accepted me like family.

I tried playing soccer, too. I met a former pro from Mexico looking to start an amateur team. So ardent was his love for the sport that I didn't mind driving a half hour each way just to be around him. But we didn't have the most committed of teams; most games ended in forfeit.

I wasn't making a lot of money, but life was comfortable.

Trying to see things glass-half-full, I made the most of my situation, and suburban life suited me just fine. I wasn't unhappy, but I knew this wasn't how I wanted to live forever.

For Justin, Lulu, DJ, Brian, and me, our early twenties were a far cry from what we had envisioned. Our moms were still weighing in on most decisions. And so when Justin proposed a three-night trip to Taipei, we pounced on the idea. We were five hungry wolves desperate for something different. This was the email thread leading up to the trip.

Justin: Bring your blazers so we can party like rock stars, Entourage style ... swim trunks as well, because we will spend our hangovers on the rooftop swimming pool in the morning.

Brian: How much money should we bring?

Lulu: Would HK$3,000 be enough? And serious about the blazer?

Justin: Never exchange money with Travelex ever again. They rip you off big time. Even local exchanges in Taipei will give better rates. Yeah man, blazers, even just for the photos. For DJ and Brian you guys will be going from work right? So you'll be in one already. Well, DJ always goes clubbing in his blazer anyway for his gentleman look.

Lulu: Are we gonna pre-drink in our hotel room? I have a bottle of vodka.

Justin: Yes. Bring the vodka.

They were kind enough to invite me, though nobody

expected me to join. The plane ticket alone would pay two months' rent. Forty hours of flying for a three-day stay didn't make sense. This was before factoring in delay and jet lag.

And yet, as information on the trip trickled into my inbox every morning, I gave in to its siren lure. That it fell on my twenty-fifth birthday was a sign I couldn't ignore. My financial situation at the time didn't allow for that kind of splurge, but I went ahead and never looked back.

Brotherhood die hard; good sense be damned.

I wanted it to be a surprise and only let Justin in on my plans.

There was only one problem—people would not commit. Justin was in. DJ was in. Brian and Lulu needed prodding. I asked Justin to do the devil's work, and he rose to the task with an unprecedented ferocity.

"Justin was hustling me harder than seniors at work," Brian later said.

With the trip falling on a long weekend, I needed to secure my plane ticket at the risk of my friends canceling. Thanks to Expedia's twenty-four-hour free cancellation, I bought a new ticket every afternoon and canceled the previous day's purchase right before the cutoff. It took three cycles before Lulu and Brian finally confirmed. God knows if that did anything to my credit score.

On the day I flew to Taipei, I rode the bus to Ithaca airport, telling every stranger about my surprise. I was the happiest boy in America. The imminent royal wedding was the talk of the town; I made a note to dedicate our first toast in Taipei to Prince William and the future Duchess of Cambridge.

But at check-in, a soft-spoken Delta employee delivered

heartbreaking news—my flight had been canceled due to a mechanical issue.

He offered a sincere apology and asked if I would prefer a full refund.

My first reaction, to my own astonishment, was relief. I could be spared from two long plane rides and a thousand-dollar hole in my bank balance, safe in the knowledge that I had tried. I could probably still go back to work.

But why had I decided to go in the first place? I asked myself. *Why had I bothered with buying and unbuying on Expedia?*

I didn't do it to tell the world I had tried.

I did it to be with my friends. I wanted to feel young, to do something irrational for once and feel good about it. If I had taken that refund, I would regret it forever. God was testing my resolve; a grounded 747 could not stop me.

Mr. Delta and I looked through every alternative, connecting through cities and airlines I didn't know existed. His frantic computer magic reminded me of the scene in *Jurassic Park* when Lex was rebooting the park's security systems to keep out a Velociraptor. I would later write a letter to Delta in recognition of his service.

In the end, he sent me off to Taipei via Philadelphia, Chicago, and, of all places, Hong Kong. It was a sign.

The surprise was almost ruined by my own hands. In transit in Philadelphia, I rushed a response to a birthday note on my Facebook wall with "Flying to Taipei to surprise my friends!" My mistake didn't dawn on me until I was thirty thousand feet above ground again. I was fidgety the rest of the flight, praying that my friends wouldn't see my post. The moment the plane touched down at Chicago, I fired up my

Blackberry Bold and deleted the post. Meanwhile, a series of emails came through from the boys.

> Brian: Happy birthday g-man. I guess we will have fun for you in Taipei this weekend. Don't worry, we'll share our stories as long as you don't mind feeling bad! And yes, Lulu, bring all the booze you can. We will either pre-drink at 7-Eleven or from our own booze. Haha.
> Justin (playing dumb): oh HAHA. What a coincidence. Didn't even realize that Gerald was still on the chain. You've been a bit quiet there. Happy Birthday and have fun celebrating in the US. BTW, does anyone think Kate Middleton is pretty? I think she's hot.
> DJ: Happy Bday, Hau Lan. We will celebrate your birthday in Taiwan as if you were there. Haha.
> Justin: DJ—can you do me a favor and buy a betting ticket at the Hong Kong Jockey Club station opposite your place? Arsenal versus Manchester United on Sunday—Man United to win. HK$500. But only if the odds are over 2x. See you at the airport.
> Lulu: Happy Happy Birthday. Yea we'll def cheers big time for you in Taipei...no worries...BTW when you make a bday wish, please wish for my stupid knee to get well soon. Kate is alright to me.

They were in for a surprise.

It was a sleepless journey to Taipei. I watched *The Hangover*, a fitting prelude to what was to come. I had a smile on my face from takeoff to landing.

The reveal didn't pan out as planned. First, I ran into DJ in the Taipei airport bathroom and tried to duck away.

"Is that Gerald?" I heard him ask Brian.

When I was done peeing, I walked up to them and said, "Oh hey, what a coincidence, guys."

They were surprised and delighted to see me.

We walked out to the luggage area to meet Lulu. He was wearing a pinstriped white blazer, a roller suitcase in one hand, and a big shopping bag of booze in another. When our eyes met, he did a double take. I watched as his bewilderment morphed into joy. He came over to punch me and gave me a bear hug. This moment alone was worth all the trouble. We hopped on the hotel shuttle and laughed all the way to the Shangri-La.

In our hotel room, we cleaned up and poured two rounds of vodka.

"To Kate," I toasted.

The rest of the night was a blur.

We arrived late at the club and watched Justin complain to the hostess for giving away our table. It was just a show; we were over two hours late.

"It's a goddamn bachelor party!" he yelled, making a scene.

Sometime during our cab ride there, it was decided that this would be my bachelor party weekend, even though I wasn't getting married. They thought this would provide an entry point for conversations—girls love a man getting hitched.

Later that night, the hostess, who had a crush on Justin and felt bad about giving our table away, bought us free double whiskey shots. At 2 a.m., those were de facto knockout punches. We poured them out when she looked away.

I danced with Brian and DJ on the dance floor. I belted out Ke$ha's "We R Who We R." Everyone looked at me like a madman, but I was on top of the world. I was with my best friends partying in Taipei. I loved the disco light. I loved people. I loved life.

But on this trip, I also saw what we were becoming.

On our final night, we left a club around 2 a.m. and wanted to end the night doing karaoke. Two Taiwanese girls were crammed in the back seat of a taxi with us. At a red light, we smashed into the front seats as our taxi halted to stop. I peered at the driver, scanning his face for cues of foul play.

"Hey, slow down. We're not in a hurry," I hissed.

He gazed ahead pretending he didn't hear me; I knew he slammed the brakes on purpose.

"No, no, hurry up," DJ snarled, his judgment softened by whiskey. "Karaoke doesn't wait."

The girls giggled.

The girls may have been DJ's friends. They may have been friends of his friends. Or they may have been total strangers. Somehow, we ended up in the same taxi heading for karaoke. Brian was passed out in the front seat, defenseless. He was knocked side to side as the taxi swerved through the streets of Taipei this early Monday morning.

My flight back to the US was taking off in six hours. Overrun by alcohol and fatigue, my body cried for bed hours ago, but my heart wanted to carry on.

After tonight, I wouldn't see my friends again for eight months.

"Club, karaoke, sleep, repeat. That's our new routine now," Lulu explained.

This is our third night; we'd become creatures of habit.

I thought about the absurdity that at twenty-five, I had known Brian, DJ, Justin, and Lulu for almost twenty years. Being with them in Taipei seemed surreal. I thought about being the odd man out not living in Hong Kong, and how many weekends like this I had missed out on.

I was coming to terms with the impending end to this trip when the driver slurred out something in Mandarin. It wasn't meant to be heard. Nobody else was paying attention. But even with DJ's drunken rambling in one ear, I made out the driver's every word. It wasn't a comment of disapproval; rather, it was said in a sarcastic resignation that made it all the more insulting.

"You Hong Kong boys are something ... Come here for the weekend ... trash our city, flirt with our girls, then go home to your lives."

At the karaoke spot, Justin ordered a king's banquet that the waiter wheeled into our room on a trolley.

"Taiwan food is good, man, even at karaoke," Justin reasoned.

Inside the room, it was every man for himself. DJ and our friend Daniel were playing drinking games with the girls from the taxi. Fresh from his nap, a ravenous Brian swept the table clean. Lulu took over the karaoke and put on a personal concert. A rambunctious Justin jumped around like a child, looking for someone to wrestle with. I was tired and jet lagged, but seeing my friends having fun filled me with happiness.

One of the girls excused herself to the bathroom. Her friend followed soon after. Neither came back. They were never seen nor heard from again.

Our karaoke sessions never used to be this wild. An occasional throwing of ice cubes? Yes. A raging gorilla trying to wrestle everyone? No. I looked around at the innocent boys with whom I used to snuggle in bed while watching *Dragon Ball Z*. They were unrecognizable, monsters before my eyes.

"You've been gone too long, man," Lulu murmured, popping a piece of deep-fried chicken cartilage into his mouth. "We've all changed."

Sitting across from Justin now at a Paris café, I ask him what he recalls from that night in Taipei five years ago.

"Are you kidding? *Ying-goi* don't remember," he says.

For him, it was just a normal night out. He doesn't even recall all the trips he has taken with the boys, let alone a particular night. But I remember it vividly. That night it felt as if I was meeting my friends again as adults for the first time. While I was starting a new life in the US, they were growing up without me.

"Why do you ask?" Justin says.

I debate for a moment whether to tell him the truth. I decide not to.

"Because I can go for some Taipei karaoke food right now."

6

GOURMET BRIAN — PARIS

AND I'D JUST LIKE TO SAY FROM THE BOTTOM OF MY HEART, I'D
LIKE TO TAKE THIS CHANCE TO APOLOGIZE...TO ABSOLUTELY
NOBODY. –CONOR MCGREGOR

BRIAN ARRIVES the next morning before we are up.

"I got so lost looking for this place," Brian hisses, wheeling his oversized suitcase into our room. He is wearing a Paul Smith T-shirt and tapered cut Levi's. His weathered Y-3 sneakers probably cost several thousand Hong Kong dollars, but he wears them casually like most people with their Nikes.

"Yeah, tell me about it," Justin echoes.

"I better warn DJ. He'll be here this afternoon," I say while texting DJ.

"Where am I sleeping tonight?" Brian asks.

I stroke the vacant side of my bed. "Right next to daddy."

I make room for him in the living room to open his suitcase. His luggage tag reads Senior Vice President at Hang Seng Bank, one of Hong Kong's largest commercial banks. His shirts are folded in perfect cylinders and lined up in uniform rows; his suitcase is like a mobile Brooks Brothers store. He must have watched Marie Kondo.

"Did your mom pack your suitcase?" I laugh.

. . .

Brian grew up in an expensive neighborhood on the south side of Hong Kong Island. We used to spend hours kicking about in his garden using flower pots as goal posts. His gardener was vocal about his displeasure, and when he complained to Brian's dad, he was always quick to give up my name. Brian's parents never made a big deal about the flower pots; it was a birthday sleepover at my house that dented our relationship. Growing up, I was allowed to stay up as late as I wanted. But not all my friends' parents shared the same philosophy.

"How are kids allowed to stay up past 3 a.m.?" Brian's mom asked when she picked him up the next morning, a subtle jab at my parents and me.

"We don't have bedtime in my family," I said, and knew right away it was the wrong answer.

Brian couldn't sleep over again until college.

Still, Mr. and Mrs. Wong treated me well. DJ and I were frequent boarders at the Wongs. Mr. Wong taught me how to eat a hairy crab, a prized delicacy enjoyed by Hong Kong and Chinese foodies in the fall. He also gave me warm water in the middle of the night during a fit of dry coughs.

After ninth grade, Brian and I both left Hong Kong for boarding schools in New Jersey. We went to different schools, but our soccer teams played each other twice a year. He was terrible at staying in touch. He never called or replied to ICQ messages. But when I'd least expected it, he'd surprise me. The winter of our junior year, I traveled to his school for a swim meet. I had sent him a message that I was coming but never heard back. It was a Saturday afternoon with three feet of snow on the ground, so I wasn't expecting much. But just as I stepped up on the starting block for my race, there he was cheering from the gallery. We spent the rest of the meet chatting and I almost missed my next race. When you really needed Brian, he'd show up.

After high school, Brian studied Business at Carnegie Mellon. He went back to Hong Kong after graduation and started off at PricewaterhouseCoopers in Audit and Assurance Services. From there, he breezed through all accounting exams and rose through the ranks. He likes name brands, but not in a flashy, in-your-face way. In fact, he is so private that he only talks about two things—soccer and Final Fantasy. We call him "Snakey" for this reason.

"You guys got big plans today?" Brian asks. He has finished repacking his suitcase.

I laugh. "Cut it out. Where do you want to go?"

He smirks.

Our day begins at Le Boeuf sur le Toit, an opulent cabaret-bar that offers Right Bank cuisine and jazz music. The name translates to "The Ox on the Roof," which is a surrealist ballet by French composer Darius Milhaud. I look the restaurant up on the Internet; my heart skips a beat when I see four dollar signs on TripAdvisor.

Fine dining is a funny business. The fancier the restaurant, the more hesitant we are to ask reasonable clarifying questions. When the waiter serves us bread without condiments, we fear that asking for butter would make us look like uncultured idiots. We gnaw on dry bread until they bring out small dishes of butter with the raw oysters.

"*Pour les huîtres?*" I ask.

"*Mais oui, Monsieur,*" he responds, surprised by my question.

I wait till the waiter turns around to start buttering my bread.

"Look at you, fancy pants. Speaking French, huh?" Brian teases.

"Oh yeah," I say with a smug smile.

I started going to French class at *Alliance Française* Silicon Valley sixteen months ago. It was two hours on a weeknight, so my devotion waned after the first month. At first, for every skipped lesson I made myself watch a French movie on Netflix. Later, when I ran out of movies to sit through, I turned to YouTube French celebrity interviews. Who would have thought Bradley Cooper could speak perfect French?

Brian's restaurant recommendations rarely disappoint. The food at Le Boeuf sur le Toit is fantastic. My delicious beef tartare confirms that I can eat that dish all day, every day.

"Brian, please walk us through what happened the other night. Ireland-Italy," I say as Justin dangles another mouthful of tender chicken breast in front of me.

"What do you mean?" Brian asks.

"What part of 'all-in on Ireland' did you not understand?" I say, raising my tone.

"Against Italy?" he laughs. "I thought you guys were still high from Amsterdam."

"We got intel on the ground!" Justin chimes in. "We were watching warm-up and stuff you don't see on TV. How could you not trust us?"

"You guys were lucky Ireland won at all. Italy hit the post."

. . .

After lunch, Brian's *tour de Paris* continues at the Hermès flagship store. He charges through the front door and beelines to the wallet section. Justin has been checking his phone nonstop and looks to be in a bad mood. Trouble with the girlfriend, I would guess. Left on my own, I watch these Asian ladies desperate to land a Birkin bag.

"Sorry, our appointments are fully booked," the Hermès employee recites in rehearsed fluency. "Can you come back next Monday?"

The ladies relent, saying something about flying home on Sunday.

I've heard about these Birkin bags from my mother. To be considered a potential buyer, one needs to be a longtime supporter of the brand. Allegedly, one needs to know people and look the part. Allegedly, there is a lengthy waitlist. Then, there is the small matter of the twenty-thousand-dollar price tag. Total insanity.

"I have a Birkin bag at home," I tell Brian with a shrug.

"No way."

"Yeah, my mom bought it years ago. It's in my closet. One of these days I'm gonna eBay it."

Brian leads us to his next stop—Chanel.

"The vintage, please," Brian asks as he makes himself comfortable in the handbag section.

"Ah," the sales lady whispers with a knowing smile. She goes around the back and fetches Brian exactly what he wants.

There are only a handful of customers here, and they are all Chinese. This is not uncommon at luxury goods stores these days. In 2013, 70 percent of European luxury goods were bought by Chinese. The term *Tuhao* (土豪), is used to describe the "uncouth rich," especially flashy Chinese tourists overseas.

Brian completes a four-thousand-euro purchase in less time than I spend on a restaurant wine list. He doesn't care about milking the experience; they must love a low-maintenance customer like him. One Christmas I went shopping with him for his girlfriend. He picked out a Burberry scarf and paid without once checking the price tag. It was HK$4,000. When he lost his Bottega Veneta wallet in Taipei—a birthday gift from this then girlfriend—he coughed up HK$3,000 to buy the same one so she wouldn't know. Is that baller or *Tuhao*?

We go back to our hotel to watch Poland versus Switzerland. Poland looks in control until Shaqiri unleashes an absurd bicycle kick. It's the kind of goal that only exists in comic books.

"Wowwww!!!" we scream in stunned admiration.

We watch the replay over and over again. With the ball popped up at the edge of the area, the five-foot-seven-inch Swiss had to generate all the power while airborne and beat the keeper at the near post. It was a supreme combination of strength, technique, and timing.

"*Bay-gao* difficult shot," I say, the understatement of the century.

"Yeah. Not hard at all," Justin echoes.

"Even DJ can do that," Brian says. When we pick teams for pickup soccer, DJ always goes last.

"Who's talking shit about me?"

We turn around and see a man standing in the middle of

the room. At five-foot-almost-eleven, his long legs are accentuated by a pair of slim tourmaline green jeans from Abercrombie. He describes himself as Luigi cute—big nose, bean-shaped head, rabbit front teeth, and dreamy big eyes that he claims connect souls. Not trying to chase the latest fashion trend for once, he has brought back the short faux hawk. He is rocking a blazer for no reason, something he started doing since turning twenty. It creates an illusion of sophistication that complements his dimpled smile. We have forgotten that DJ is arriving today.

"You scared the shit out of me," I say.

"You guys left the door open," DJ shrugs.

"DJ, looking dapper man," Justin says. "Getting ready to meet some white babes?"

He shrugs. "Nah, I have my own white babe now." He is referring to his new American girlfriend.

I study his nose up close. He broke it a few weeks ago playing soccer; I've been waiting to tease him about it.

"So the doctor couldn't do more?" I tease him.

"Haha, yeah I was begging him for a proper nose job."

DJ almost didn't join us on this trip. First, he made up a bullshit excuse about wanting to study law abroad instead. Then, he confessed that the whole trip was planned so much around Euro 2016 that it didn't make financial sense for a non-soccer fan like him. He only plays soccer when called upon to make the numbers.

"Financial sense? Non-soccer fan? This is about brotherhood!" Justin lectured.

That didn't work.

"Alright. What if we do Formula One racing in Europe?" I asked.

He said he could get behind that.

He went ahead with his research and came back with several options. He even put it down on our itinerary and coordinated the transportation. But no one else was interested. So DJ decided to go by himself. He did his driving this morning in the UK before taking the train to Paris.

"How was the track?"

"Pretty good. The car was 150 brake horse power with a 1.6-litre engine. Zero-to-sixty in 4.3 seconds. One hundred-forty-five-mile-per-hour top speed; four-speed gearbox," he rattles off the numbers.

If he is bitter about us flaking, it doesn't show.

"So how does it work?" I ask.

I don't really want to know but think it is polite to show some interest.

"They give you a thirty-minute briefing on track driving technique. And then you have a fifteen-minute driving session. Around ten laps, three behind pace car. "

"I see. Is it worth doing?" I ask.

"Definitely. But the track is for athletes only," he says.

I laugh. "Where do you come up with these one-liners?"

In our pajamas, we snuggle in bed to watch Croatia against Portugal. Croatia is favored going into this game on the back of a big win over Spain. Portugal displayed flashes of brilliance against Hungary in the last game, but remains winless in the tournament. As expected, Croatia has Portugal on their back foot right from the start. Deep into overtime, Croatia has a flurry of chances. When Cristiano Ronaldo wins the ball back, rather than booting to safety, he launches an audacious counterattack. The Croatian keeper makes a brilliant reflex safe to deny Ronaldo, but can only watch as Quaresma taps in the rebound to send Portugal into the Quarter-Final. The entire Portugal squad storm the corner flag in celebration. They have stunned the Croatians, half of which are still in the Portugal half.

"Woohoo! We'll get to watch Cristiano in Marseille!" I cheer.

So now Poland and Portugal? More exciting? My mom texts me immediately.

Of coz. C Ron, I write.

The one that looks like you? she asks.

I wish, I reply.

I turn around, but DJ and Brian are half asleep.

"Ten years ago, we landed in Lima at 1a.m. and went straight to a pub until closing," I say. "This time, we arrive on a Saturday night in Paris and go to bed at eleven."

"We're becoming old men," DJ sighs. Brian and Justin nod.

We had youth on our side in 2006, but some things come easier now with age.

First, our family's approval.

In 2006, we each asked our families for a ten-thousand-US-dollar travel budget, a nice round number we pulled out of thin air. We had no clue how far that would get us, or the hard work it took to earn it in the real world. It caused rumblings among DJ's older brothers that the youngest one always seemed to receive special treatment. Brian likely faced a fair dose of backlash, but he kept family problems private. Justin's dad's discontent was born more out of principle. Uncle Wong, who had long questioned our character, was less than pleased when one of my emails found its way into his inbox. We had an email thread going among us, but somehow our parents got added to the distribution. Under the subject "Around the world summer 06," I made plans about sipping skinny margaritas in the Caribbean, seducing tropical maidens, and indulging in other comforts in life that we hadn't earned. I might have mentioned "experimentation" in Amsterdam even though we didn't end up going there.

"Hey next time, let me read the email before including my dad," Justin said.

Such was our naivete about the world and reality. In the end, we did not quite ask for their permission so much as expected their approval.

Though my father was lukewarm about the idea, my mother's unequivocal support bankrolled the trip. She loved to travel and never had the chance to do that until later in life.

"You have the rest of your life to work," she said.

My harshest critics turned out to be my friends. The idea of foregoing a summer internship was ludicrous in their minds, what with the competitive job market.

I told them what my mom said.

"That was like thirty years ago," they replied. "Nowadays everyone has a degree. Good luck finding a job."

In the end, I took the road less traveled. Ten years on and gainfully employed since graduation, I am proud to say that, for once, my mother was right.

BRIAN'S LIST OF TOP 10 RESTAURANTS

(IN NO PARTICULAR ORDER)

Sushi Kado (Hong Kong)
L'Atelier de Joël Robuchon (Hong Kong)
8 ½ Otto e Mezzo Bombana (Hong Kong)
Amber (Hong Kong)
Steak House Winebar + Grill at Intercontinental (Hong Kong)
Sushi Mori (Hong Kong)
La Terrasse (Saint-Tropez)
Seryna (Tokyo)
Florilège (Tokyo)
Clancy's (Los Angeles)

7

KONG BOYS — LYON

BEHIND EVERY GREAT MAN IS A WOMAN ROLLING HER EYES –
JIM CARREY

OUR DAY BEGINS in a dire crisis at 6 a.m.

"Shit. My suitcase's full," Brian yaps.

The Chanel came in a big gift box. A classic, First World problem.

"Just throw the box away," I moan, enraged that Brian has chosen now to repack his suitcase.

"But she likes the box," Brian replies. "Well, just gonna tell her it didn't come with it."

"Shut up," I laugh. "You're terrified of her. Remember Kenting?"

This past April, we took a trip to Kenting, Taiwan for the Spring Scream Music Festival. At a beach party sponsored by Tinder, Brian was posing for picture with the Tinder cutouts when a pair of promoter girls photobombed him. The girls asked to be Facebook friends.

"Sure," Brian said.

Later that night, he opened Facebook to the notification of "you are now friends with..." He clicked onto those girls' profiles and screamed.

"Oh my God. I'm screwed. I'm so screwed," Brian cried in panic.

He showed me the Facebook pages of the promoter girls. Full nudes plastered the screen.

"No more boys trips again if Meg sees this. Shit, shit, shit ..." Brian screamed as he smashed the unfriend button.

Starting in Paris, we will drive 470 kilometers south to Lyon today with a "quick stop" at La Vallée outlet mall for Brian. Another five-hour drive tomorrow will bring us to Monaco on the southern shore of France. From there, we will cruise along the Côte d'Azur to Saint-Tropez the day after. Our last stop is Marseille, where we will meet up with Dave, Kenny, and Sho. A lot of driving ahead, but also many exciting places to see.

We stuff our rental car to the roof and bid Paris goodbye.

"Let's take a selfie," DJ says.

He is in the driver's seat holding up his thumb. Justin offers a barely-there smile with his three-day stubble. Brian sticks his head out from the back and is clearly not ready for the shot. I'm not even in the picture as I'm texting in the backseat sorting out our game tickets to the Quarter-Final.

La Vallée outlet mall is just an hour outside of the city. By mid morning, eager shoppers have already filled La Vallée's parking lot.

"Let's check in at the visitor center first," Brian commands. "They give out special discounts."

Another day, another shopping extravaganza for Brian.

"How many times have you been here?" I ask.

"Hmm ... Several? This is my third Paris trip in five years."

"You never mentioned that to us, *gwai-su*," Justin says.

Gwai-su is the act of covering up dishonest behaviors. Examples of *gwai-su* include going after a girl without announcing to the boys, traveling out of country without telling anyone, disappearing during clubbing, and taking people's ex-girlfriends out for lunch.

We split up. Justin goes into Moncler; Brian checks out Paul Smith; DJ and I saunter around window-shopping. Some bigger stores have long queues outside just to get in.

"So how's it with the new girlfriend?" I ask. She is a Floridian who moved to Hong Kong to teach. They met through dating apps and started seeing each other shortly after.

"It's good. We're still trying to get used to each other," he says.

"What's she like?"

"Has a strong opinion and isn't afraid to stand up to bullies."

"Just like you. Do you guys argue a lot?"

DJ is one of the most argumentative people I know. This trip won't end without he and I getting into some passionate debates.

He laughs. "Sometimes. 'Heated discussions,' I would say."

"So she loves Hong Kong? Is she a party girl?"

"No, not at all. She wakes up early on weekends to go hiking and stuff."

"Damn, how did she end up with you then?"

He shrugs.

"She's not materialistic at all. For our first date, I suggested a cheese fondue dinner. She said, 'sounds good, but we don't have to go somewhere so fancy. Casual is okay too.'"

"Haha. But did she know that the cheese fondue dinner is actually at your apartment?" I laugh.

Where some people reserve special outfits or fragrances for hot dates, DJ has his cheese fondue set. All his past flings who dared step foot in his apartment have had their run with that puppy. Like they say in *Anchorman*, 60 percent of the time, it works every time. Romance ensues.

DJ has offered to host a fondue meal for the guys.

"No thanks," we always say.

I have known DJ since we were six. Baby DJ was cute in an up-to-no-good way. In our childhood class photos, he stood out as the troublemaker, always making faces or finding ways to stand out. He had the world fooled for the most part; Brian's mom was particularly fond of him, a fact she liked to impress upon me often ever since the sleepover incident. From day one I saw DJ for what he was—a silver-tongued monster with an unwavering love of women. And we love him for who he is. We love him for his unflinching candor; we love him for his thick skin and capacity to withstand ridicule. When you need a travel companion, look no further.

DJ describes himself as a mild narcissist, a hopeless romantic, and a social chameleon. I've met many of DJ's girls over the years. I used to host an annual Christmas party. Each time, DJ brought a different girl. One year it was the tall, skinny girl who threw up all over the dance floor at the after-party. She's the mother of a two-year-old now. There was the girl who worked in finance. She gifted me a bottle of Moët Rosé but didn't strike me as interested in DJ. There was the girlfriend who threw a fit over a pair of stilettos DJ had promised to buy her; they broke up soon after. There was the flight attendant, whom, at least from what I saw, DJ actually liked.

After completing his degree from UC Berkeley, DJ also considered staying in the US. He found little luck in a difficult job market and moved back to Hong Kong. He has lived there since, unhappily at times. One day, he sees himself moving back to the US to raise a family.

"I will be an awesome dad who tells terrible dad jokes," he always tells me.

We squander four hours at the outlet as Brian puts his credit card limit to the test.

"You guys done already?" he replies on the group thread. He appears to be offended by our efficiency. "What? I thought we weren't leaving till 4 p.m.? I still have to go to Burberry."

"Go! Go! You have one hour!"

Justin meets DJ and me for lunch at a nearby Japanese/Chinese restaurant. I haven't been doing a good job keeping up with my mother's messages. Every time I check WhatsApp, I find multiple correspondences in which she poses questions that she answers herself later in light of my nonresponse. This reminds me of the saying, "Give a man a fish, and you feed him for a day. Teach a man to fish, and you feed him for a lifetime." By ignoring my mother, I am teaching her to fish.

She's in Italy at the moment, getting excited about the Portugal-Poland game in Marseille. Today's WhatsApp questions revolve around how to stay safe during the game.

"Any colors to avoid?" she asks.

"No."

"Are you sure?"

"We're watching a soccer game, not going to war."

"But didn't you see the news last week? The Russian and English fans."

"Yeah, so? These things happen."

"I don't want to get in a fight."

"No one is gonna fight you."

"Hey assholes," Brian sneers when he shows up at the car, begrudging a shopping session cut short.

We have been waiting in the car ready to go.

"How far is Lyon?" Justin asks.

"About four hours," I say, confirming on my phone.

We stop midway in Auxerre to watch Ireland versus France. All the restaurants and bars are closed. The fourth largest city in Burgundy, Auxerre boasts only a population of forty thousand, 39,999 of whom are at home watching the game today. The only person working is the receptionist at the Ibis hotel, but even he's not all there in spirit.

"Can we watch the game here?" I ask him.

He nods mechanically. His mind is elsewhere.

We huddle around the tiny lobby TV and set up base to cheer on Ireland.

Coming off the victory against Italy, Ireland faces their toughest opponent yet. But unlike the last game, the boys in green are playing without their strong support base. Rumor has it that many Irish fans had to go home after running out of travel funds. Even they didn't expect their boys to make it this far. Against these staggering odds, Ireland strikes first through a penalty. The Irish outplay and out-hustle a frustrated French side and go into halftime with the lead.

"Where's Justin?" I ask. He has disappeared.

"On the phone," Brian points to the room in the back. "He was the one who wanted to watch the game."

Brian and I look at each other and shake our heads.

"Just like you last time," I tease Brian.

"Haha, very funny," Brian says.

During our last trip, while we were traveling the world, Brian's mind was with a girl back in Hong Kong. This was long before smartphones when it took triple-tapping the "two" button to text the letter "c." But the inconvenience of an analog phone was no obstacle for Brian's resolve. He was tight-lipped about everything, but we all knew it was his long-time childhood crush. She was four years our junior, a substantial gap considering our smaller denominator back then. We knew nothing about her, and often wondered whether Brian was in love with her or the idea of her—the mystique that none of us knew about her. They would go on to date. We would know her as Little Tiff.

After three years in Upstate New York, I spent a year in Boston for graduate school. During that time, I got to know Little Tiff, who was finishing her undergrad at Tufts. Her romance with Brian had ended by then, but she still welcomed me to her parties. She was a nice girl; we could have been good friends.

"I wasn't as bad as Justin now," Brian says in defense of his 2006 texting frenzy.

I would agree. Even though Brian was always on his phone, he at least had the decency to keep things under wraps. Justin is unapologetic. At halftime, I go to the back room and check on him. I find him with his headphone on and phone raised to eye level, smiling into the screen like a pervert. I shoot him a "c'mon man" look, which he ignores. I've been texting Molly too, but FaceTiming is reserved for the down-time, not during prime-time group activities.

France emerges a different team in the second half. They storm to the lead through a quick-fire double from the hottest man in world soccer—Antoine Griezmann. When Shane Duffy denies Griezmann's hat trick at the expense of a red card, it's a long way back. The final score line should have reflected a larger margin had Gignac remembered his shooting boots.

"Justin, we're leaving," I yell as we walk out of the Ibis lobby. We wait in the car and keep glancing at our figurative watch. After ten minutes, there's still no sign of Justin. As someone who detests tardiness, I find it obnoxious that he has no qualms about making people wait.

I run back in and shout across the room again.

"Okay, okay, just a minute," he yells.

I consider our options.

"Should we just leave his ass here?" I ask.

Brian and DJ chuckle. "It wouldn't be the first time."

On our last trip, we had a ten-hour layover at Buenos Aires airport. Brian, DJ, and I decided to wait it out at the airport and watch the World Cup. Against our counsel, Justin and Lulu went into the city to shop instead. When it came time to board, they were nowhere to be found.

So what did Brian, DJ, and I do?

We boarded the plane, and felt pretty good about it. We thought it was justice served.

Sitting in the dimmed cabin next to two empty seats with

a fifteen-year friendship hanging by a thread, we asked ourselves—were we out of line? What if something bad had happened to them?

In the end, I made peace with our choice.

A normal friend would have held the plane up at all cost. A good friend might have thrown his body across the gate to stop it from closing. But only a true best friend would have done what we did; we begged the airline staff for immediate departure, and took it upon ourselves to direct passengers during boarding, much like firefighters orchestrating an evacuation. We knew that deep down Justin and Lulu would have wanted what was best for us, and what made us happy. Our story would be all the richer for it. And so, we followed the path to maximum happiness—Margarita Island for the most fabulous four days of our lives. When Lulu and Justin turned up midway through our dream Margarita run, what I felt was disappointment. To this day, I still haven't figured out why. Perhaps I felt that they didn't deserve a place in paradise, having abandoned us in the first place. Perhaps we worried they would steal all the girls.

I didn't feel bad abandoning him ten years ago, and I don't feel bad about it now. Every second we spend waiting in the car, the image of Justin FaceTiming burns deeper into our memory.

But we can't leave him here. Not by himself.

When he finally sashays out of the hotel with an infuriating lack of urgency, the damage has been done. He tries to make conversation, but we return one-word responses and afford him no eye contact.

Though Justin always talks a big game about brotherhood, he has a history of choosing (mmm ...) girls before bros. In

Kenting, he was a partial participant all three nights. He disappeared for hours on end without disclosing his whereabouts, textbook *gwai-su* behavior. We confiscated his phone on the final night, but he somehow managed to steal it back. Such was the man's determination.

When we confronted him about it, he denied it.

"What do you mean I was on the phone? I was with you guys the whole night partying!" he said.

Thankfully, our friend Kenny, a lawyer, had been collecting photo evidence. When Kenny unleashed the incriminating photos, we all rejoiced at having nailed Justin— here was one of Justin texting at a bar, sucking a lollipop; here was another one of him texting, with my bathing suit in the background.

We were at the airport huddling around a small table when Kenny released the photos.

"If you really zoom in," Sho said, holding his phone up close, "you can actually make out what Justin was typing."

At Sho's urging, everyone started zooming into the pictures on their devices.

"I think this one reads 'Thank you babe' ... hard to tell," Brian said.

"I think you're right," Dave echoed. "The last word was definitely babe. Let me try the one above."

"Are you guys playing Hangman?" Justin yelled, wishing he could snatch all our phones at once.

"If you squint, you can probably see clearer," Sho said. "Just like when you try to watch a censored video."

Every time DJ takes over at the wheel, he drives like he has something to prove. He leans into the turns like a race car driver. The more I ask him to slow down, the harder he steps on the gas pedal. Hurtling along at 180 kilometers an hour, the car rumbles even on a pencil-straight road. Justin and Brian are rocked back and forth in the back like Bauhinia trees during a Hong Kong typhoon. How they manage to sleep through this is a mystery to me.

"I don't even drive this fast in video games," I say, hoping DJ will take the hint.

"It's Europe," he shrugs. "Look—I'm following the traffic pattern."

Sometimes I don't know how DJ and I are friends. His driving has been a constant contention between us. On our Italy trip, I tried everything to get him to slow down, including threatening to jump out of the car. In Kenting, he insisted on renting a real motorcycle for himself even though everyone else was riding slow electric scooters. He is selfish in his pursuit of speed. We are two diametrically opposite people. I find people like him a menace to society; he thinks I'm a wuss.

Needing a distraction, I put on some music. First up —"Achy Breaky Heart."

"Is this country music?" Justin asks.

"That's right," I say in my best attempt of a southern drawl. "It's Miley Cyrus's dad."

"Ah ... It's catchy."

I smile, turning the volume dial clockwise. "Let's pump the bass on this bad boy."

Not to be outdone, Love Song Little Prince takes over soon after with a few English jams of his own. We have forgotten about the fact that we were mad at him.

"Check out this Adele song. I almost cried the first time I heard it. It's called 'All I Ask,'" Justin says.

We have no choice but to listen. It's not a bad song, and I can see how it could grow on you, but the tears aren't forthcoming.

"You guys aren't paying close enough attention to the lyrics," Justin reasons.

We arrive at Pouilly-le-Monial just before sunset on a fine Sunday evening.

"I guess we're here ..." I mumble, double-checking my phone GPS. The boys look dazed by our rural surroundings. We are parked on top of a golden hill shimmering under the setting sun.

"Country retreat, huh?" Brian asks.

DJ climbs out of the driver seat and stretches. "Gerald, where are we?"

I shrug. "I don't know man. I just picked something close to Lyon. The Airbnb pictures looked nice."

I also picked it because it is cheap, but they don't need to know.

A silver-haired woman in a flowery ball gown steps out of her walled cottage. "Are you Gerald?"

"Hi! You must be Elisabeth."

From the many glamour shots around her house, we learn that Elisabeth is a former beauty queen and an avid skier. Now in her sixties, she's an empty nester.

"Here's the bathroom ... There are three beds on the loft. Please make yourselves at home," she says with measured excitement. "My husband is out of town."

Gulp.

"Hmm. Is there a supermarket around here still open?" Justin changes topic. He is already thinking about dinner.

"Sunday night? Ah no. This is France."

She calls one of the nearby restaurants to make dinner reservations for us. We thank her and head over to Oingt, a beautiful French village built of golden stones in medieval times. *La Vieille Auberge* is an unassuming Lyonnais restaurant restored from an old stable. The menu is in French, and with us being the only English speakers here, ordering becomes an exercise of faith. On the owner's recommendation, chicken liver pâté, Lyonnais sausage, and other Burgundy specialties are brought to our table.

"Try this," Justin cuts a piece for each of us. "Can you taste what this is?"

We cannot, but later find out that the dish is called *quenelles de brochet*, a pike cake served in a creamy crayfish sauce.

We also open a bottle of Beaujolais. Described by wine expert Karen MacNeil as "the only white wine that happens to be red," the Beaujolais's light body and high acidity goes down easy with our heavy dishes. It's not considered an expensive wine, but I find it refreshing. Brian takes a picture of the bottle label.

"Brian, you like this?" I ask, surprised that a ten-euro bottle finds its way into our food critic's illustrious gastronomic resume.

"No. I'm taking a picture because I probably won't drink this ever again in my life," he says with a candor I find both innocent and snobby.

Roses are red,

Violets are blue,

Brian's an elitist,

What can you do?

Molly sent me a video of Lupe playing with sprinklers; I commit the cardinal CB sin of watching it on my phone at the dinner table. Besides being cheap, a CB is also someone who plays with his phone while other people are talking.

"Is that your dog?" Brian asks.

"Yeah, she's a puppy."

"What's her name?"

"Lupe. She's the dearest thing to me in the world."

"Including your girlfriend?"

"Including my girlfriend (It's a joke babe!)."

Justin shares a dog story of his own.

"At home, we have a dog that I've been trying to befriend for a while. One day I went to a pet store. 'What's your tastiest dog treat? I need to do some serious bribing,' I said to the owner. He sold me this beef tendon stuff. I went home and did some bonding with the dog. That shit works. He was very sweet; so I thought we were boys."

He takes a sip of Beaujolais before continuing.

"Then one day, he was gnawing on a bone when I walked by. I went to pet him and he bit me. I yelled at him. Like really yelled. Like how I yell at people on the soccer field but with curse words. I told my maid and apparently she had been bitten several times already. She said that when the dog has food with him, you can't get close, even if you're just passing by. He won't even give up the bowl; my driver figured out a way to refill his food with a stick. Later, I found out that this dog actually killed a cat at his previous home. So we adopted a killer."

Justin doesn't say what happened next, but I doubt he tried to win the dog over after that.

We return to our quaint country retreat after dinner. Though we have only rented the loft, Elisabeth gives us free rein to the whole house. She says she'll sleep in the smaller cabin because, again, her husband is out of town.

Her home has a Beauty-and-the-Beast quality to it. Sofas blanketed in white sheets, cracked photo frames, growth charts in the children's room, a wobbly foosball table, and an out-of-tune baby grand piano are all relics from happier days. DJ, a profile picture connoisseur, recognizes endless photo opportunities here. First, he poses at the piano doing his best Jay Chou impression. Next, he perches at the easel channeling his inner Picasso.

My own Facebook days are long gone; DJ is still at the peak of his game. His last profile picture update took social media by storm. Within hours of its release I was made aware of it by no fewer than four sources, one being Wendy, my cousin, and a hi-bye friend of DJ's, at best.

"Your friend. LOL," she captioned.

It was all she had to say.

When I first laid my eyes on the photo, I thought it was DJ's grandpa in his youth. It was shot in black and white with a graininess emblematic of photos from the sixties.

"We used a special filter at the studio," DJ would later tell me. "Each shot took over an hour."

Locking eyes with the subject in the picture for the first time, I came to understand the reason for all the social media commotion. Leaned slightly forward and with his face turned forty-five degrees, DJ's steadfast gaze breathed life into this candid shot. The implicit caption read, "Do you want to dance?" I didn't even notice that his blazer was open and he was bare chested.

For days we ridiculed him, both in his face and behind his back. We gave him a new nickname—Model.

And that wasn't the end of the story.

What he posted on social media was only a cropped version. On one of my later trips to Hong Kong, I stopped by DJ's place before dinner. When he was in the bathroom getting ready, I browsed on his computer to kill time. And there I saw the original. To my horror, it was a full body shot with no pants on.

All he was wearing was the blazer.

I closed the file quickly.

"Who took those studio pictures for you?" I asked later.

"My friend and his wife," he replied.

Some relationship he has with this couple.

There is no TV or alcohol at Elisabeth's, so we stay up till 2 a.m. playing cards and listening to Jay Chou's new album on repeat. When we're tired, DJ and Justin claim the single beds in the living room, leaving me with the familiar devil in Brian on the double.

For all the accolades Hong Kong enjoys as a city, critics don't have many nice things to say about the people. Hong Kong children especially have a bum rap. They label us spoiled city boys raised by overprotective parents. The first time I stayed over at *Goo-ma's* house during boarding school, she correctly pointed out that I had never done any housework. Most of my friends grew up with live-in maids who did all the cooking and cleaning. Our maid even helped me with my homework. She was like a second mother to me. In many ways, she knew me better than my real mom.

Today, out-worked and out-competed by our brothers on the Mainland, Hong Kong children are looked upon as whiners.

They even have names for us.

A "Kong boy" is indecisive, unambitious, and whiny who tends to bow to his girlfriend's whims; a "Kong girl" is materialistic and idealistic. She sees an affluent, good-looking, caring, and successful boyfriend as her inalienable right. She is to be treated like a princess.

While I find these stereotypes unfair, sometimes we make it easy for people to form them, like when we leave trash everywhere at Elisabeth's house. There are empty water bottles and plastic packaging all over the first floor, the part of the house she has let us use for free.

"This is not the Grand Hyatt, guys," I say, hoping they sense the seriousness in my tone.

The excuse? There's no trash can in the house.

"Don't be mad," Brian throws his arm around my shoulders. "Check out what I got for you."

On his phone, he shows me a collage of pictures he took of me while I slept. Are these pictures supposed to calm me down?

Lyon is the third most populous French city and a vibrant cultural and gastronomic center. It is also the meeting point of two major rivers—the Rhône and the Saône. The former runs from Switzerland to southern France and has served as an important transportation channel since the Roman times.

"Wow, check out that car," Brian says, pointing at a parked BMW with a broken rear window.

You can still see shards of glass on the back seat and all over the ground. The car has been broken into.

"I thought these things only happen in video games," Brian adds.

"In Hong Kong, when you put stuff in your car, it's generally assumed safe," Justin echoes.

Growing up in one of the safest cities, we are foreign to the perils of the real world. At least the intruder had the courtesy to pick the smallest pane as point of entry. Honor among thieves.

We end our short stay in Lyon with one last Lyonnais meal. We give *quenelle* a second chance and arrive at the same lukewarm conclusion. Justin's Lyonnais sausage comes wrapped in a thick bread that tastes like vodka. I have no complaint about my escargot. I order *foie de veau Lyonnaise* as my entrée, even though I'm not a big veal fan. My dish comes on a giant plate. A thin, big piece of meat rests on top, blood seeping out in all directions. I cut into it and realize it is actually veal liver.

Justin cringes.

"How is it?" he asks. He doesn't eat organs.

I think for a minute.

"Raw, juicy, and wrong."

8

GAMBLE AND DRIVE — MONACO

EVERYTHING I LIKE IS EITHER ILLEGAL, IMMORAL, OR
FATTENING. –ALEXANDER WOOLLCOTT

"HEY DJ, can you steer for a second?" Brian asks.

"Ok, I got it," DJ says, leaning over from the passenger side.

"Whoa, whoa, what are you guys doing?" I yell as Brian tries to fish his phone from his pocket. "Snakey, are you texting Meg!?"

"Need to place bets on the games. Huge comeback tonight!"

We are going through a start-stop construction zone but still.

"Give me the phone!" I yell. "I'll do it!"

After an "unlucky" losing streak, we are down to our last HK$15,000.

I sigh. "If we lose all the money before Kenny, Dave, and Sho even get here, we'll never hear the end of it."

People visit Monaco for a litany of reasons. Picturesque beaches, beautiful women, jaw-dropping yachts, supercars, the Grand Prix, casinos, and the spectacular views, all make this place irresistible. But for DJ and me, we return with a revenge narrative.

We made a stop here eight years ago on our backpacking trip. Prior to Monaco, we had spent two weeks on the road rushing through every "must-see." We just wanted to let loose, and hoped that a night in Monaco would provide the spark we needed. In our only button-downs, we took the last pleasure train from Nice into wonderland.

From the Monaco train station, we pranced along a coastline that screamed new money. We thought the entire city would be littered with clubs. Maybe we were looking in the wrong places; we traveled from one end of the city to the other before finding one. It also never occurred to us that drinks would be so expensive. We were on a budget. With the euro trading at 1.4 against the dollar, a cocktail cost thirty US dollars. We couldn't justify splurging on alcohol when our daily food allowance was ten euros. Patrons in the club were exclusive, especially against non-French speakers. These were no doubt the future Rich Kids of Instagram. Their tables had an endless supply of Grey Goose. Sober and desperate, DJ and I moved from place to place and stood around, nursing our complimentary Long Islands till they were warm to the touch. We tried to make friends, but ended up watching them step away one by one as our self-esteem dwindled to a flicker. At 3 a.m., we cut our losses and left.

"But this time it'll be different, right DJ?" I say.

We are a bigger army. More important, we have our own money now.

"I can't get a signal," DJ says, frowning as he fiddles with his phone. "Brian, did our roaming package not cover Monaco?"

Even with GPS, navigating around Monaco is challenging. We drive around in circles in search of a turn that doesn't seem to exist. On our third go at this roundabout, it dawns on us that our destination lies beyond a police roadblock we've been avoiding. We pull up next to two very good-looking police officers. The male officer speaks no English; his female colleague does all the talking. She explains that this is an entrance for Le Rocher residents only. I explain that we are renting a room from a Le Rocher resident. I hand her our paperwork. She has nice squoval nails.

"How much are you paying a night?" she asks.

Maybe she is considering Airbnbing her place too.

I tell her I don't remember, but around a couple hundred.

"Drop off your luggage and then park the car in the garage at the bottom."

It is not what we want to hear. Because of traffic, we have already missed most of the Spain-Italy game. And with Italy taking an unexpected lead, our big bet on Spain is hanging by a thread. I knew letting Brian gamble and drive was a bad idea.

We send Justin and Brian to the apartment first to will the game back in our favor. DJ and I will get the car parked and get it over with.

"Do you know where to go?" DJ asks as we try to navigate down from Le Rocher to the designated parking garage.

"No. Let's ask that policeman. Pull over."

There is no car coming from either direction, so DJ pulls into the opposite lane to talk to the officer. The moment we cross the double solid lines, the officer starts blowing his whistle in rage and signals for us to pull over. He looks so distressed that it is almost comical. For a moment, I think he is going to show DJ the red card. He comes up to the window on the driver's side, takes a deep breath, and adjusts his Ray-Bans. Uh oh, here we go.

I offer a megawatt smile; DJ doesn't seem to take my cue.

"Yes?" DJ says, rolling down the window and barely making eye contact.

"What is this line?" the officer asks in perfect English, pointing at the double solid line.

Conversations that begin with a rhetorical question are destined for disaster.

I frown on the inside but offer a sweet smile.

"Yes, we saw," DJ begins to explain, "but ..."

"Then why did you drive over the line?"

And so his sermon begins.

He goes on and on. We nod and nod like two Japanese feng shui cats.

"Just apologize," I mumble in Cantonese.

"I'm sorry ..." DJ whispers.

It works. In the blink of an eye, the policeman turns to me with a warm smile.

"How can I help you?"

In Chinese theater, a *Bian Lian* (變臉) performer changes his or her personality with a swipe of the fan. This Monaco policeman would make a great *Bian Lian*.

It takes us half an hour to park the car and make it all the way back to Le Rocher. We sprint up to the apartment and almost kick in the door.

"Did Spain come back?" DJ and I ask, trying to catch our breath.

Justin lowers his head. His body language resembles that of a surgeon in movies stepping out of the ER with bad news for the family.

"All or nothing on England-Iceland!" Brian bellows, his hair messier than I last saw him. He is beyond *lawng* at this point.

We change into our best party outfits to head out for dinner and watch the game. But we can't figure out a way out of Le Rocher.

We are on a big hill, so walking is out of the question.

"Let's take the bus," Brian suggests.

No one has a clue where to get off, and by the time we realize that the bus is traveling in the wrong direction, we're deep in the dead part of town. We run from restaurant to restaurant in frantic search of a TV showing the game.

"Everything's such a rush," DJ complains.

I ignore him.

"We didn't factor in driving five to six hours a day into our itinerary," he adds.

That finally sets me off.

"Why don't you plan it then next time?" I snap, but deep down I know he's right.

Justin and Brian are staying a safe distance out of the line of fire.

When we backpacked in Europe eight years ago, DJ and I fought all day, every day. We argued on practical matters, like whether his laptop was safer in his suitcase or backpack. We locked horns over meaningless philosophical debates, like who was more talented—Cristiano Ronaldo or Clint Eastwood? I took positions on issues based not on my own beliefs, but on whatever DJ disagreed on. We disagreed fundamentally on how fast he should be allowed to drive. I mocked him for not knowing how to eat fish with bones; he belted out a scornful laugh when I messed up our hostel booking in Venice. Our relationship became so acrimonious that toward the end of the six weeks we spent more time apart than together. On days we did spend together, he would rather set his camera on a timer than stoop so low to ask for my help. We brought the worst out of each other. Our friendship survived, but it took months before things went back to normal. Eight years later, we are in Monaco inching closer to that breaking point again.

At long last, we find a beachfront restaurant showing the game. I see DJ shaking his head as he studies the menu, probably because of the price. I know we are getting ripped off too, but I'm ready to punch him in the face.

We scarf down some mediocre Asian fusion food and plop ourselves in front of the TV. I've had enough of DJ's complaints that turning my back to him is my idea of "taking the high road." Still I can hear his incessant complaints to Brian, this time about the speed of the free restaurant Wi-Fi. I know he's uploading photos. He has no interest in soccer.

"I want to restart the router," he whines.

I want to restart you.

I am indifferent to DJ's problems because I am preoccupied with my own. With England trailing 1–2 after an all-action opening twenty minutes, we bet big on a comeback. They can't lose to Iceland, right?

"Come on, England!" Justin cheers through gritted teeth.

As a lifetime England fan, he has been down this road many times before. I have looked down on England my whole life. Today, with my financial interests hinging on their success, I finally get a taste of Justin's chronic frustration. Captain Rooney looks a shadow of his former self. The pace and strength that once made him a powerhouse have deserted him. Operating in central midfield where space and time are at a premium, his careless and predictable first touch betrays him time and again. Once a prodigy mentioned in the same breath as Ronaldo and Messi, his star has fallen hard and fast.

We storm out of the restaurant at the final whistle. Iceland slays the Three Lions.

"Brian, how much do we have left in the fund? I want to withdraw my shares," DJ says.

"Sorry, withdrawing is not an option," I reply, not making eye contact with him.

Brian doesn't respond. Justin plods ahead with his head down. The succession of defeats has extinguished the fire in our belly. We trudge along like four broken men to loveless marriages back home. We feel stupid dressing up thinking we would be partying tonight. Even near the end, we allowed ourselves to believe in a fairy-tale comeback. Maybe the Saint-Tropez beaches tomorrow can turn things around. At least the European Championship gets a day off.

I have a few unread messages from my mom.

Are we sitting together at the match, she asks, referring to the Quarter-Final in Marseille.

Yes. Us and my friend Kathleen, I reply.

How's Monaco, she asks.

It's ok. Not much to do. Just seeing stuff, I reply, not ready to talk about our setback just yet.

Driving to Porto Venere now. See you in two days, she writes.

She is taking a road trip of her own through Italy and

France. She sends me beautiful pictures from Cinque Terre and is clearly having a better time than us right now.

We lost HK$11K (~US$1.4K) in three hours. The cracks in our relationships are beginning to show. Partying is the last thing on our minds. And DJ can't find a phone signal. We dawdle along the beach of Monaco, which, thankfully, is free. Eventually we find our way to the Casino de Monte-Carlo.

"Gerald, remember this park?" DJ asks at the Jardin du Casino.

"How can I forget?" I smirk.

Eight years ago, after our hugely disappointing night at the Monte-Carlo club, we had hours to kill before the first morning train back to Nice. We were sitting on the benches at Jardin du Casino when an Eastern European man walked up to us. He was wearing skintight jeans and a white button-down that flaunted his lush chest hair.

"Want a massage in my hotel room?" he asked in heavily accented English.

"Emm ... no thanks," DJ replied.

"No, no," the man explained, "*you* give massage."

DJ and I looked at each other.

"Wait, you mean for money?" I asked what I felt was an important clarifying question.

"Yes, yes. How much?" he rubbed his fingers for the universal money sign.

DJ and I looked at each other again.

"Get out of here," DJ said to the man.

The only time we ever agreed on anything.

Fast forward to 2016, and here we are sitting on the same bench.

"Sometimes I wonder what would've happened if we'd said yes," I tell DJ.

"I would have beaten the shit out of you, that's what," DJ says.

I laugh. "If he came back tonight maybe we could make back the eleven K we just lost."

We laugh out loud for the first time since this morning. Whatever the contention, humor always diffuses it for us.

I remember Monaco a little differently. Last time despite the disappointment, DJ and I still came away with fond memories. We were swept off our feet by the opulence. This time, the magic of Monaco seems to have waned. Everything feels old and tacky. Maybe the excesses on social media have desensitized us. Maybe our bar has been raised.

"Gerald, why did you insist on coming to Monaco again? You and DJ have been here before, right?" Justin asks.

I just shrug. The truth is, I was hoping that the flashy cars, champagne, super yachts, and crazy parties would motivate us to work hard. I want us all to have a good life and enjoy together.

I look out to the stunning shoreline of nighttime Monaco, still ruing trusting England with our money. *What were we thinking?*

Monaco: where dreams go to crash and burn.

Tired, broke, and emotionally abused, we return to our high-efficiency studio. I have always fantasized living in one of these—a two-hundred-square-foot man cave catered to one's basic survival needs. You walk through the front door into a living room that also serves as the kitchen. The bathroom is tucked in a corner. A twin bed is up on the "mezzanine," accessible only by an industrial wall ladder. It reminds me of the forts my brother and I built with blankets and pillows when we were kids. On my own, I would have fallen hard for the studio's rudimentary appeals. Sharing it with three full-grown men, though, ruins the romance of it all.

"Good thing Dave, Sho, and Kenny aren't here," I say, trying to imagine squeezing even more people in here.

"Well, we would have rented a different place in that case," Brian says.

"Or two of these," I counter.

"How was the shower, Justin?" DJ asks.

"Can't turn. The shower curtain sticks to you. Now I know how Android 17 felt when Cell absorbed him," he says. A Dragon Ball reference.

I'm next.

I quickly come to appreciate the difference a few feet can make. The shower drain is clogged, so I wrap up business quickly before flooding the place.

An anxious Brian waits on deck.

"Don't worry, I was careful with the soap," I tell him on the way out.

Brian, normally generous and easygoing, has only one pet peeve—poor bar soap etiquette. When DJ and I used to sleep over at his house, we showered together every night. Brian had one strict rule—never, ever, rub the communal bar soap on your privates. Three ten-year-olds cramming his parents' shower stall? Perfectly fine. Genital contact with the bar soap? Cardinal sin!

The wood floor disappears once we pull out the bed. Brian and DJ share the twin bed on the "mezzanine." We figure that if someone were to fall off, Justin would do the most damage; first law of Physics—F=ma.

"Which way are you supposed to sleep?" Brian asks as he sizes up the bed. Sleep the long way, you're a half-turn away from a seven-foot drop. Sleep the short way, your legs dangle off the bed.

"They should write instructions to this place," DJ says.

I scavenge around for pillows and sheets, an easy enough task with only so many places to look. I find two pillows without cases and a duvet without cover. We use the felt blanket as an improvised mattress cover. We will come to learn that it's impossible to fall asleep on something with so much traction.

"Hey Brian, I'll trade you my pillow for your cushion," Justin proposes.

The offer seems too good to be true. Brian drops his cushion from above before Justin changes his mind. Justin smiles. He throws a T-shirt on the cushion and goes to sleep. The pillow wouldn't have fit. He seems satisfied with himself.

"Good job," I say. "You're Jason Bourne."

"Guys, it's clogged," DJ announces. He is the last to shower.

"The shower, right?" we ask.

"No, the toilet."

"Shit," Justin squawks. "I ate curry tonight."

9

ATONEMENT — SAINT TROPEZ

YOU'RE ONLY AS GOOD AS YOUR LAST HAIRCUT. –FRAN
LEBOWITZ

THE WHATSAPP TOPIC du jour is Snexit ("Snake" + "exit").
News of yesterday's gambling setback has our shareholders in
Hong Kong screaming. When we see them in person
tomorrow in Marseille, there'll be a lot of explaining to do.

I wake up around seven and can't fall back asleep with the
arctic breeze of the air-conditioning in my face. I change,
pack up, and go for a walk; fresh air and alone time will do me
good. Le Rocher, or the Rock, is the oldest part of Monaco,
where the prince resides. Last night was the closest I'd ever
come to being a prince's neighbor. Le Rocher offers a dazzling
view of Monaco's coastline, a fact that I decide not to share
with DJ to ensure a reasonable departure time. Outside a real
estate office, I notice an ad for a unit identical to ours listed
for a cool 1.2 million euros. One-point-two-million euros for
a two-hundred square-foot apartment. Who can afford to live
here?

With a moment alone, I decide to catch up on my journal.
When my friends are around, there's too much distraction,

which is an ungrateful thing to say because they were the reason I started writing.

There are moments when one becomes a writer.

Haruki Murakami found his calling at a baseball game. "The satisfying crack when the bat met the ball resounded throughout Jingu Stadium," he wrote in the introduction of *Wind/Pinball*. "Scattered applause rose around me. In that instant, for no reason and on no ground whatsoever, the thought suddenly struck me: I think I can write a novel."

I too recall my precise moment. It was ten years ago in Machu Picchu. I was head-down scribbling in my notebook in the ruins when I almost tripped and fell on my face.

"Are you going to write a book about us?" DJ asked.

I shrugged. I hadn't decided what to do with my notes yet. The idea of writing a book fascinated me, but it called for more discipline than I'd ever demonstrated. Scribbling in my journal was one thing; turning it into a book I could be proud of was quite another. Since boarding school, I hadn't so much as written my name in Chinese, so English was my only vehicle. But with a pedestrian SAT verbal score to show for, the odds were against me.

Justin's next comment changed everything.

"I don't think this can be a book," he said. "We aren't interesting enough for people to read about."

An idea formed in my head. Perhaps defiance was what made me a writer.

When we went back to Hong Kong, I spent the rest of the summer transcribing and editing my journal. I added photos and created a pdf ebook that I shared with our friends. To my surprise, people actually read it. Most of them read the whole thing in one sitting, often at the office during their summer internships. People found our antics sassy and funny. My mother even had hard copies printed. I gave it the fitting title —*Wannabe Backpackers*.

I didn't stop there. The following summer, I found a publisher in Hong Kong who believed in my project. On a cool evening in March 2009, I flew back to Hong Kong and joined family and close friends for the book launch in the Helena May, a private women's club in a declared monument on Garden Road. I had a script written up for DJ, Brian, and Justin on what to say, which they read with no inflection whatsoever. It was otherwise a lovely evening of celebration with our loved ones. We even made it in the *South China Morning Post* the next day under the heading "Intrepid (sort of) Quintet Launch Book about Trip to Faraway Lands."

"Wow, what a turn out!" my publisher said to me as a long line formed for the book signing.

"They're mostly here for the party. Maybe two of them will actually read the book," I mumbled.

Though the book didn't exactly fly off the shelves, it changed my life in many ways. I discovered my passion for writing, which I found engaging and therapeutic. I made new friends from writing groups. Book readings became my favorite events to attend—from internationally acclaimed bestsellers to local authors grinding for their breakthrough. My newfound passion for literature led me to a local book club where I was the only male participant. In my first session, the book of the month was Elizabeth Gilbert's *Eat, Pray, Love*, a woman's memoir that resonated with millions. Everyone had something profound to say, reading passages from earmarked copies and drawing on experiences of their own. I knew I couldn't contribute in any meaningful way. So when it came my turn to weigh in, I stood up and said, "*I wish Giovanni would kiss me. Oh, but there are so many reasons why this would be a terrible idea.*" They all laughed that I could recite the opening from memory.

My fellow Wannabe Backpackers found other uses for my book. It made for a great conversation icebreaker and a perfect second-date gift. Hundreds of copies were distributed to that end. To my surprise, girls found our travel struggles endearing. Even our parents seemed eager to promote a book that celebrated our childish antics. My father, of all people, was the first to notice when the link to my website stopped working. Coming from him, this was a compliment of the highest order. Like many Asian parents, he is frugal with his money and praises. One time, I won the club championship at my golf club. When I sent him a picture of myself with the enormous trophy, arguably the crowning moment for my limited golfing talent, he wrote back—*the size of the trophy seems disproportionate to the relevance of the occasion.*

I didn't dare seek out Justin's dad's feedback after the pre-trip email faux pas, but his mom was our biggest cheerleader.

"At one point," Justin once told us, "my mom had a whole box of your books in her car and just gave them out to her friends and their daughters at the golf club. I had girls message me out of the blue saying they've read the book."

Maybe these girls should thank me for giving them an in to reach out to Justin.

Back in the Monaco apartment, my friends are slow to leave.

"Guys, I need to drop a deuce," Brian warns from the mezzanine.

"Please don't," all reply in nervous unison. The last thing we need is more poop in a clogged toilet.

He barges into the bathroom anyway.

"*Bay-gao mo-bun*," Justin says.

Mo-bun literally translates to "no manners." It is a polite way to call out inconsiderate behavior, something my father would say when he sees trash left behind on a public picnic table. Losing eleven K yesterday, we can forgive (Yup. Brian is taking the fall for that one.). Stinking up the whole apartment? No chance.

He emerges ten minutes later. "I guess the toilet fixed itself."

We breathe a sigh of relief.

We slam shut our suitcases, style our hair to perfection, and make our slow descent to the parking lot.

DJ is taking the first shift at the wheel. He stops the car at the garage gate looking for something.

"Did you keep the parking ticket, Gerald?" DJ asks, turning all his pockets inside out.

"You have it, right?" I ask, checking mine too.

"I must have tossed it out yesterday..." DJ stammers, his voice trailing off.

I shake my head and get out of the car to pay the twenty-euro fine.

"DJ, you're paying me back," I say definitively.

He snorts, puts the car in gear, and peels out of Monaco.

DJ's misfortune continues. This time he drives into the wrong tollbooth.

"*Ding*, we don't have auto-toll in this car?" he complains.

"Dude, we've been driving this car for days. You know this," I say, relishing every moment of his struggles.

With cars piling up behind us and honks blaring in the background, he presses the panic button on the machine and reads out his credit card information to the operator.

"Pierre ... Ying Shu ... Lam. Y-I-N-G ... S-H ... Yes American Express. Three-seven-eight-five ..."

It is the longest minute in our lives.

DJ completes his hat trick of miscues at the next toll booth. He finds the cash booth this time, but a simple coin drop into a toilet-bowl-sized basket gets the better of him.

"*Digh-sei* (抵死)," I say. The phrase, which means "to deserve to die," is used when people get served what they deserve. We aren't going to forget this one for a while.

Today we celebrate Justin's thirtieth birthday.

Ten years ago today, we flew from Miami to Nairobi, with a ten-hour layover in London. An airplane cabin was no place to celebrate a milestone birthday. I was the trip organizer, and not a day has gone by this past decade without me longing to right that wrong.

My atonement will come via Le Club 55, the most exclusive club in Saint-Tropez. Le Club 55 requires reservations months in advance, and like many exclusive establishments, it only takes phone reservations. So I bought credit on Skype and called them at 5 a.m. California time and spoke in broken French.

"*Em ... bonjour. Je veux ... emm ... faire une reservation ... pour l'anniversaire de mon ami ...*"

These small inconveniences, I was certain, were God's way of letting me repent for my original sin.

I knew little about Le Club 55. I was expecting red carpet, bouncers, and guests lining up around the block.

Wrong.

You can't see into the club from the outside. In fact, we drive by it twice missing the small sign. We leave our car to the valet and make our way into the restaurant.

"Wow ..." we exhale, taking an immediate liking to the open-air atmosphere.

The place is not glitzy like Vegas beach clubs. There are no neon lights, loud music, or scantily clad waitresses. Instead, Le Club 55 offers a homey, laid-back appeal. Under a big canopy held up by bleached driftwood, we settle into the cozy outdoor dining area on white furniture and baby blue linen. Even on a stifling day like today, the misting fans keep us cool. This place is exclusive and elegant without being pretentious.

On the hostess' table, we find a handwritten card with "Gerald" next to the table number.

"Take a picture of this if you want to show off on Instagram," I tell DJ.

The food is exquisite. Perhaps our only regret is not ordering the vegetable platter, which appears to be a popular dish. Whole reddish, cauliflower, bell peppers, mushrooms, cucumber, carrots, fennel, celery and artichokes are served straight from the garden on a wooden cutting board.

"That platter would've been great for the pictures," DJ says.

We raise our rosé flutes. "Alright Justin. Happy Thirtieth!"

In the US, a typical thirty-year-old is married, sometimes even with kids. Living with parents at this age is frowned upon. In stark contrast, if you own your own home in Hong Kong at thirty, you either have rich parents (again) or have made a killing during investment-banking heydays. Often, you need both. These days, new homes on Hong Kong Island sell for HK$20,000 to HK$30,000 per square foot. For a five-hundred-square-foot apartment, HK$10 million is the starting price. Even a parking spot can cost HK$2 million to HK$4 million. For a fresh college graduate taking home HK$11,500 per month working at a Big Four accounting firm, how is home ownership attainable?

Because owning a home is such a distant dream, many don't even try to save up for a down payment. The path to home ownership will come through a winning lottery ticket, a giant inheritance, or an improbable change in Hong Kong's housing climate. And because staying at home comes with free meals, utilities, and laundry, the entire paycheck can be spent on partying. Who is thinking about marriage when they can live like rock stars?

Not many of our friends are hitched. We have perfected a litany of excuses on why we're still single. On a practical level, most people can't afford the wedding, or the ring, or the exorbitant cost of Hong Kong housing. On a spiritual level, a soulmate can be hard to come by, what with the glamour and distraction of Hong Kong. And on a perception level, my delusional friends and I still maintain that cool kids don't tie the knot this early. All our heroes—Cristiano, Zlatan, Conor McGregor—are either bachelors or lead lives to that effect. Among our close friends, only Phil is married; we call him Uncle Phil these days. Being married precludes you from doing things like going on a three-week boys' trip.

With each passing day, our excuses grow pettier. DJ talks about marriage sometimes, though I suspect the regular sex is the main appeal. He is adamant that he would make a great father one day.

"Honestly DJ, I can't see it," I say, emptying my flute and signaling Brian to refill.

"Trust me. I'll be a cool dad."

Justin jumps in to gang up on DJ. "How old will your son be before you start bringing him to clubs?"

It's hard to picture ourselves as responsible parents. Only yesterday we were flying down the freeway at 180 kilometers an hour, shaming each other for clogging the toilet, and gambling away eleven K. But little by little, looking back, we are smoothing the edges of our youthful arrogance.

"When I went to my first job interview, I had long, brown hair and a fake diamond earring. So *On-gou*," DJ shakes his head. *On-gou* is a Cantonese swear word that translates to "stupid penis."

"Well, my first job interview, the guy asked me why I didn't want to stay in Investment Banking after my internship. I just said, 'it's too hard, man.' He gave me that look that said I probably should have lied," Justin says. "Then at another interview when they asked me about past leadership experience, I talked about the thousand-people ragers I threw in college. He wasn't impressed."

My mom tries to call me. I send her to voicemail.

Can't talk. At fancy restaurant, I text.

She sends me a play-by-play of her road trip, and asks if she needs her passport for the game because she forgot to bring it.

No need, I write back and put my phone away.

Here without our fifth Wannabe Backpacker, our conversation drifts to Lulu's inexplicable absence.

"Did Lulu tell you guys why?" I ask.

Headshakes all around.

I first broached the subject with him last summer when I stopped by Hong Kong for work.

"You're coming, right?" I asked Lulu during a heated game of FIFA at Justin's.

"Mmm ... I don't think so."

I paused the game and looked at him in stunned silence.

"What do you mean 'don't think so'?"

He needed time to think this through, I thought. He was never the quickest to sign up for anything, but he always showed up in the end. I thought about how much it would take for me to miss this trip. Work? I got my boss's permission two years in advance. Death of family? Maybe. A pandemic? That'll probably do it.

I brought it up again in Christmas. He had a new excuse this time.

"I booked a trip to Thailand with my girlfriend. She's renting a private villa to celebrate my thirtieth birthday," he said, twiddling his thumbs.

I was beside myself.

"You're skipping our trip to go to Thailand?" I said, holding back from yelling.

I love Thailand, but you can go for a long weekend, not in lieu of our big trip.

"Yeah I know, but she already booked it ..."

I interrupted him. "We booked this ten years ago!"

He had nothing else to say. Neither did I.

It didn't make sense to me. Maybe he was planning a surprise late entrance, I thought, or he had legitimate reasons that would become clear in due time.

Later, when I saw the following WhatsApp exchange on

the night of Justin's birthday banquet at the Hong Kong Club, I thought maybe we'd found the answer.

> Lulu: Thanks for the dinner guys. I just landed back in Canada. See you guys in a few months!
> Sho: We miss U Lulu. Don't worry—your sister is in good hands while you're gone (evil emoji).
> Dave: Oh you're moving to Canada Lulu?
> Kenny: Yeah sad stuff. He's gonna disappear again for a while.
> Lulu: Dave—I've been gone for a few months.
> Brian: He only flew back for Justin's birthday.
> Lulu: Yeah, such a hectic weekend trip to HK but totally worth it.

I spent minutes trying to process this information amid a flurry of emotions.

Canada? Lulu? He was the last person I would imagine ever moving to Canada.

To fly back just for a friend's birthday was unlike Lulu. Improbable though it was, I felt a glimmer of hope. Of course this was why he couldn't come on the trip. Thailand was a cover-up for his secret move to Canada for reasons he couldn't share. He would never turn his back on us on his own accord. His Facebook profile picture was still the book cover of *Wannabe Backpackers*. It felt like solving a math problem I already knew the answer to—it was right in front of me all along.

I messaged Brian. "No wonder Lulu isn't coming on our trip. He moved to Canada without telling us!"

"Dude, it was a joke man," Brian replied. "Sho made that up

to make fun of Lulu for never being around anymore. And Lulu played along in the group chat. He didn't actually move to Canada."

If my feelings toward Lulu had been disappointment before, all that remained now was lost hope.

Sitting here at Le Club 55, the four of us speculate his real reason.

"Maybe he's mad we call him names," Brian says.

Sometime last year, Lulu was caught at a restaurant with Dave's ex. When we confronted him (lovingly) about it, we found out that he'd been keeping in touch with many of our exes behind the scenes. I do believe that he reached out to them more to right our wrongs than for his own romantic aspirations. After all, everyone loves Lulu. Though these secret friendships were platonic to our knowledge, we still gave him a new nickname—X-man (Ex-man). He even has his own emoji — the one with crisscrossed arms.

"No. I bet his girlfriend hates us," Justin says.

For no good reason, Lulu once brought his girlfriend along on a boys' night out at club Magnum. This was back in 2014 when we were at our marauding worst. Some nights we made Justin Bieber look like a saint. Can you blame her for not wanting Lulu near us?

We are all disappointed Lulu missed the trip. Disappointed for us, and disappointed for him.

"When our families get together in the future and talk about this trip, Lulu's kids will ask 'Dad, why don't you have anything to say?'" Justin says, imitating a baby's voice.

"Maybe he won't even come to the dinner," Brian says.

"Whatever the reason, things will never be the same between us," Justin says.

At this moment, it is hard to argue otherwise.

Le Club 55 springs to life in early afternoon.

Everyone looks famous or rich here. There are a lot of good-looking patrons around. They laugh the confident laughs reserved for people who have cracked the secret to life.

"Another bottle of rosé?" our server asks.

A typical Le Club 55 lunch, we are told, doesn't end on just one bottle of bubbly. Though this is Justin's big day, we aren't the day-drinker types.

"I think we're okay. Our friend DJ here prefers a natural high," Brian says.

"DJ, how did you teach yourself natural high?" Justin asks. "I have seen you go to clubs and instantly get into the mood dead sober."

DJ takes a sip of water and explains. "Well, I was partying and drinking a lot in college and eating junk food all the time. I was really abusing my body. My senior year I started getting this really bad pain in my stomach."

When we were in Europe after graduation, his stomach pain flared up on occasion. One time, he even collapsed on the floor at the Marseille train station after an espresso.

"I saw a doctor and he said it was ulcer. 'Absolutely no alcohol,' he told me. Well, I was twenty-two and I wasn't going to sit out and watch you guys party, right? So I kept partying sober and mind-tricked myself to get in the mood."

"Haha, were you faking it?" Brian laughs.

"No. The funny thing is, when people around you are drunk and happy, you feed off that euphoria. It's very strange!"

"This is a feel-good story of human adaptability," I say.

After his recovery, he decided not to revert to his old ways. He still takes a whiskey shot or two on occasion, but only with certain people. Entering our thirties now and feeling the weight of every hangover, we are all envious of DJ's special gift.

After lunch, we are invited to enjoy the cobalt blue water at the restaurant's private beach. It's hard not to fall in love with this place. I like to think I have made up for ruining his twentieth birthday. If a platinum French blonde were to throw herself at Justin, my penance would be complete.

Catching sight of DJ screwing a portrait prime lens onto his trusted Nikon D610, Justin and I wander off quietly, leaving Brian as his designated helper. He hands Brian the camera and sashays out to the pier like it's *Project Runway*. There are families all around us, but DJ pays them no attention. Back, front, sitting down, standing up, arms spread, arms crossed, shirt on, shirt off ... DJ monopolizes the pier until every permutation is exhausted. Waiting for their turn at the pier, a family of six looks on in disbelief.

"He's a model," I explain, backing away from DJ to establish distance.

We feel somewhat out of place around the family scene here, so we decide to check in to our Airbnb and hit up one of the public beaches later this afternoon.

An Airbnb veteran now, I have come to appreciate the convenience of hotels that we take for granted—parking, 24/7 reception, privacy and much more. Airbnbs require coordination with the host. And there is always waiting involved. To check in to our place in Saint-Tropez, we have to sneak our car into a gated community and wait for our host to let us to the building.

"Brian and DJ—why don't you guys get the car parked? Justin and I will take the luggage and wait for our host," I say.

Justin and I drag our suitcases to outside the building lobby and rest under the shade. It is a short distance but we've already worked up a sweat. To our surprise, DJ is already there waiting for us.

"You parked the car already? Where's Brian?" I ask.

"We can't open the gate," he says without lifting his head to look at us. He's sitting on his suitcase and editing pictures on his phone.

In other words, DJ abandoned his post.

I walk back to the car and find Brian fuming.

"DJ's supposed to go with me. He just disappeared!"

"Yeah, he's playing with his phone in the lobby now."

"So *mo-bun*."

Thirty minutes later, a French lady walks up and identifies herself as Mireille. She looks to be in her seventies; her skin is tanned from a happy life on the beach. Her place is a major upgrade from our Monaco residence. It is still technically a studio, but everyone has his own bed. Justin is excited about the kitchen and the two-door refrigerator.

"The shower and toilet are separate. Just like Amandine's place," I say.

"Makes sense," Justin nods. "Just think about our situation last night."

"Is there Wi-Fi?" DJ asks.

"No Wi-Fi," I reply.

"What? How can you book a place without Wi-Fi?" DJ looks to me for an explanation. I have none.

"Hey check out this fridge," Brian says. "There's a little door in front that lets you reach in without pulling open the whole door."

Brilliant, efficient, and lazy as hell, this fridge must have been designed by a beer drinker.

I slide open the glass door to the beach view. "Let's go swimming."

Brian and DJ go to get changed. I wait till they're out of sight to give Justin his present.

"Happy Birthday, man." I hand him an envelope. "Hope this is on your bucket list."

Inside is a piece of paper on which I scribbled, "You and your guest are cordially invited to WrestleMania 33 in Florida on April 2, 2017." And then on the back, I added—"floor seats."

"Holy shit," he shrieks. "I'm going to frame this."

When I go to concerts and sporting events myself, I always buy the nosebleed seats. This is the most lavish gift I've ever given. I thought long and hard about what to give him. In years past, we have never really done presents. But this year being our thirtieth, he got me something special. A mysterious package arrived on the morning of my birthday. It was a WWE Replica Blue Winged Eagle Championship Title Belt. I knew who it was from right away. It came with a note.

Happy big 30 bro. I may believe that I am better than you at beer pong, football and foot golf. But in my eyes, you're still a champ.

I hadn't followed WWE since the late nineties, but I appreciated the meaning behind it nonetheless. The belt weighed over five pounds, and after a quick research on Google, I was shocked by its price tag.

I spent days racking my brain on what to get him back. He had everything, and I wanted to get him something meaningful and lasting. I decided to reach out to Vincy for ideas. I didn't have her number, so I asked Lulu for it. They had gone to the same high school.

Gerald: Yo, give me Vincy's number.

Lulu: For what? U're interested in Vincy too?

Gerald (shaking my head): Yes. Just give it to me.

Lulu: Justin will kill you. lol

Gerald: No. I need to get Justin a birthday gift. Need some ideas.

Lulu: How is it related to Vincy???

Gerald (jaw drop; shaking my head more): Dude, they are dating. Where've you been?

Lulu: Oh shit! I didn't know!!! OMG.

Canada.

"Are we sure this is the right way?" I ask the group.

We've been looking for the beach at Quartier de la Bouillabaisse for a while.

Then, three topless girls cross the street with the swagger of champions.

"Guess this is the right place," DJ smiles.

Tops seem to be prohibited on this beach. Some girls are just hanging out with their friends; others parade around with their heads held high, flaunting their assets.

"I guess we can sit down for a beer here, right?" I ask.

"Mmm ... only if we have to," Justin echoes.

"Brian—stop staring." I slap him. It's not easy to go about business as normal under these conditions.

We pause for a moment to find our bearings. On our right is the gorgeous Côte d'Azur; on our left stands a long line of bars challenging us to a Saint-Tropez bar crawl.

Challenge accepted.

The first beer disappears in record time. For once, we're not racing daylight or worrying about gambling losses. We don't have a care in the world. The cavalry is arriving tomorrow. Life is good.

When we reach the last bar, we break off for some personal time. Brian FaceTimes Meg. DJ wants to meet some people. I take a dip in the ocean. Justin blasts Chinese music from his phone. As I'm doing backstrokes in the open sea, I watch DJ pace back and forth trying to talk to a tall Asian girl. His tentative body language doesn't look promising.

"DJ, did you talk to her?" I ask when I get back to our table. Ninety percent of the time he chickens out.

"I forgot to throw her a glance when I walked past," DJ explains.

Head drops and chuckles all around. That's DJ for you; there's always some excuse.

"Guys," Justin rises to his feet and pumps his chest." I've decided to make a dinner for my boys tonight."

"Really?" we ask. "What's on the menu?"

Justin winks. "You'll see."

Justin discovered his culinary passion from an episode of *Entourage* where Johnny Drama makes scrambled eggs with soy milk for his brother. Justin aspires to be the same adorable, protective, and nurturing chaperone for his boys. With a full kitchen at our disposal tonight, this is his chance.

"I want to play the role of a boarding school head chef for the evening and cook a value-for-money yet deluxe meal that will also save us from being ripped off at a fancy restaurant in Saint-Tropez," Justin declares.

I never knew Justin to be the role-play kind of guy.

At the grocery store, Justin picks up ingredients for his secret dishes. Brian and I wander off to pick up daily essentials. It's not every day you buy shampoo and body wash in a foreign country. So when the opportunity presents itself and a brand called Playboy is on offer, you buy it.

"No, no, no," Brian barks, snatching Playboy from my hand and placing it back. "We're not kids anymore."

"But Mommmmm," I clamor.

"Come on, let's go. I'll buy you sour laces." He leads me away from the shampoo aisle.

We love sour laces. When we were kids, they were sold at the Happy Valley soccer field for a dollar each. After each soccer game, Brian and I would buy a full bag and share them. Nothing beats binging on sour laces while reliving the key moments of the game.

"These laces suck," I say. "They stick to your teeth."

"Yeah, the middle part is too hard. The salt is sour enough though."

We see a tall girl at the supermarket. As if on cue, we start singing 高妹 (tall girl), a Cantonese song from the early 2000s about winning over a taller girl.

We are on the same wavelength.

"Justin, are you ready to go?" we yell from the cashier.

He was last seen lurking somewhere in the seasoning aisle

looking for oregano, parsley, basil leaves, and other "key spices."

Justin emerges with two full baskets of grocery. He can't keep a smile off his face.

"Don't pretend you guys never grocery shop to cook for your girlfriends," Justin says.

Dinner preparation begins in full force the moment we get home. Brian mans the chopping station; I prepare a garden salad. I open a bag of prewashed salad mix and pour it into a bowl. Done.

Head chef Justin labors over his secret dishes.

"What's with all the suspense, man?" I ask.

"Yeah. Give it up already." Brian tries to peek into his grocery bag.

"A home appliances brand Sunbeam hired neuroscientists to perform research," Justin says. "They found that women are more aroused by men cooking than using power tools."

We laugh.

"Is that what you learned from your MBA?" Brian asks.

"Now you have DJ's attention," I say.

DJ has no time for our nonsense. He is setting up his camera tripod to capture us dicing onions and feeding each other scraps, luxuriating in every bite. He has the camera on a timer and shuttles back and forth, alternating between cameraman and model.

"Wow, I look terrible without a shirt on," he frowns scanning through the pictures. "Better start over."

Forty-five minutes later, Chef Justin unveils his two courses. First is bouillabaisse, a Provençal rockfish stew with saffron, orange rouille sauce, and croutons—the soup equivalent of a paella.

"The flavors are much richer than what we had in the Lille restaurant," I say.

"I used the entire one-pound bag of mussels and clams. Don't want to go all CB when cooking for my boys," Justin says proudly.

"So *lawng*," I say, relishing every bite.

"Well to be honest, my phone ran out of data so I had to freestyle. I definitely went for quantity over quality."

The second course is linguine with garlic and chili. The pasta is cooked al dente and doused with a healthy serving of olive oil and garlic. Everything is delicious and I wish I had a bigger stomach.

After dinner, we play cards on the rooftop to savor every drop of France's long summer days.

We play a game called Big Two, the most popular card game in Hong Kong. Each player starts with thirteen cards and take turns playing them into the discard pile. The first to get rid of all your cards wins. At the beginning of each set, the person who goes first can choose to play a single, a pair, a triple, or a five-card group (straight, flush, full house, four of a kind, straight flush). The next player must play a better hand with the same number of cards established by the previous player, or pass. The set ends when three consecutive players pass, at which point the person who played the last card begins a new set. It is called Big Two because Two is the highest card. The game is fast-paced and prone to big swings.

A player is "shut out" when the game finishes without being able to play a single card. Shutting one opponent out is rare enough. Shutting out all three almost never happens. In tens of thousands of games I have played, I have only seen it once.

DJ achieves just that tonight.

"Shut out all around! In your face!" DJ explodes, slamming his cards on the table in dangerous euphoria. I'm not sure I've ever seen him happier. We're all hysterical—DJ because of his perfect victory, us in spite of total defeat. France is great, but it's this stupid laughter that we'll remember for life. Where is the tripod and camera to capture this priceless moment?

The next morning, we stay in bed and do our morning rounds on Facebook.

"What time are Kenny, Dave, and Sho arriving today?" Justin asks.

"After lunch. We'll meet them in Marseille," DJ says.

"Enjoy this last morning of peace, boys," I say.

"Oh my god," Brian says. "Check out the videos they just uploaded from their flight here."

Occupying the middle bulkhead seats, they pulled down the tray table and set up shop for beer pong. They named the videos "Mile-high beer pong champs."

I sigh.

Since beer pong's introduction to Hong Kong a year ago, bars and clubs have been riding its massive popularity. Businesses are innovating how the game is played and monetized. They have digital beer pong tables these days that track player profile and performance. They interact with your phone via Bluetooth, and display your alias on the overhead screen for everyone to see. Leave it to us to turn everything into an arcade game.

I like beer pong, but for me, these transformations have stripped the game of its original beauty.

In college, beer pong was cool because it was the forbidden fruit. When we were freshmen, beer pong on a

Friday night required many steps. First, an upperclassman needed to buy the beer. Then, we had to take down the closet door and make a table with two chairs as legs. All this at the risk of a Resident Assistant walking in and writing us up for drinking.

I am also not a fan of how the game has institutionalized. The tables in Hong Kong are always regulation length. A referee keeps time. And you don't even drink out of the beer pong cups! When your opponent sinks a cup, the referee pours you a separate drink to the precise, agreed amount.

My fondest beer pong memory was when a bored group of guys sat in front of the TV and spontaneously decided to "pong." Our table was a slightly warped particle board propped up on two industrial-sized trash cans. Someone ran to the store to buy red Solo cups and ping pong balls. Half the shots ricocheted off the overhead lamp until everyone adjusted to the playing conditions. The whole night we smack talked and accused each other of cheating. When you got shut out (i.e., losing without sinking a single cup), you had to run a naked lap around the house in the snow. You drank straight out of the cups, pubic hair and all. It was raw, makeshift, and unsanitary, but that's what made it fun.

Brian made lunch reservations at La Terrasse. If Le Club 55 was exclusive and casual, La Terrasse is all-out luxury. Located at the five-star La Résidence de la Pinéde, La Terrasse serves only a handful of customers out on an open terrace. In starched white shirts and black neckties in double Windsor, the waitstaff carries the professionalism of Iron Chef contestants. They exude a quiet confidence and

attend to our every whim without coming across as disin-
genuous.

"Our server looks like a cross between Scarlett Johansson
and Ronda Rousey," I say. Justin can't stop staring at her with
his heart-shaped eyes.

She responds to everything "with pleasure." When she
notices that DJ is taking pictures, she brings out a velvet foot-
stool for him to set his camera on. Talk about attention to
detail.

"I feel unworthy to be served by this gorgeous, wholesome
girl," I sigh.

"Their bouillabaisse costs fifty euros," Justin says, probably
reliving his boarding school chef fantasy.

Under white umbrellas, we enjoy the view of the hotel's
private bay. The lawn is freshly manicured. Every course is
meticulously arranged on our plates. Our waitress looks like
an action-movie star. We are dining like royals.

The only other customers in the restaurant is this Asian
family of three. We are too far away to eavesdrop, but their
mannerism feels too familiar. The father is on his phone
texting. He makes no eye contact with the server when his
entrée is brought to the table. The mother has big Gucci
sunglasses on. She summons the restaurant manager and
points at her salad. The son is playing his Nintendo 3DS and
has hardly touched his sixty-euro cheeseburger.

"It's so easy to spot rich, spoiled Hong Kong people," I say.

Brian nods. "I bet they're saying the same about us. We
probably look pretty *Fu-yee-doy* now, too,"

We like to think we belong to a less pretentious echelon of
society. Justin dines at Michelin-starred restaurants, but he
also enjoys microwaved dim sum from 7-Eleven. Before club-

bing, Brian always pre-drinks at home or at 7-Eleven. I only shop for clothes on sale. DJ walks thirty minutes to work every day. We can stretch a dollar if needed, especially when it is just me and DJ.

On my last trip to Europe with DJ, our go-to meal was a one-euro McDouble, sometimes two if we splurged. Every few days we devoured a whole Margherita pizza for five euros, seven if we wanted toppings. When we ran into two old Hong Kong schoolmates in Florence, they brought us to a buffet dinner for a whopping fifteen euros. We fasted for twenty-four hours right before to get our money's worth. All told, I came home thirteen pounds lighter, an alarming loss for someone who only weighed 140 pounds. Our moms thought we were sick.

Hungry though we were, shoestring travel was romantic in many ways. On an overnight ferry from Naples to Sicily where we couldn't afford a sleeping cabin, DJ and I lay out on the deck under the stars, passing a cheap bottle of Chardonnay back and forth. We cherished the generosity of others and hoped that one day we could reciprocate. It was hard for us to imagine then that we would be dining at places like La Terrasse with ScarJo making steak tartare right in front of us.

"I spent ten years planning Justin's birthday, and Brian's casual lunch has upstaged that," I concede.

JUSTIN'S BOUILLABAISSE RECIPE

.

1. In the pot, sauté onions, tomatoes, leeks, and garlic in hot oil
2. Add white wine and let it boil
3. Add as much water as you want (we added way too much)
4. Add spices (bay leaf, ground pepper, saffron, chili flakes, etc)
5. Add an appropriate quantity of frozen mussels (or the whole bag)
6. Add an appropriate quantity of frozen scallops (or the whole bag)
7. Let it cook until your boys are hungry

10

FIST OF FURY — MARSEILLE

GO TO HEAVEN FOR THE CLIMATE, HELL FOR THE COMPANY. –
MARK TWAIN

WE SUCCUMB to a severe food coma after lunch at La Terrasse, terrible timing for the person who has to drive to Marseille.

"Who's driving?" I ask.

No one says a word.

I guess I am.

I snatch the car key from DJ and plop into the driver's seat. I hear snoring from the backseat before we even pull out of the parking lot. What I would do to switch places with them. My eyelids weigh a thousand pounds.

Two plates of truffle fries was a bad idea.

Aside from my brief fallout with DJ, this has been a successful road trip. We have driven from Paris to southern France in four days without incident. I need to stay strong on this final leg to bring it home. In Marseille, we will get to spend two nights at the same place to rest up. And maybe Sho, Kenny, and Dave will inject new energy to the group. If we get there early, maybe I will have time for a nap before meeting my mom for dinner tonight.

I turn the stereo up to drown out their snoring and tighten my grip on the steering wheel.

Lean back and close your eyes, the devil says.

I try to will myself awake. It is bumper-to-bumper with no end in sight. The three o'clock sun, which felt punishing only moments ago, is now cradling me into sleep. I am fighting a losing battle. Forget drinking and driving—eating and driving is far more dangerous.

Then, I hear a whistle.

Two six-foot tall French policemen motion for me to exit at a roundabout. I slow down and pull over.

"What's going on?" DJ asks. Everyone is wide awake now.

The officers walk over to our car, aviators and all.

"This road. Ninety kilometers per hour," one of them barks, scribbling "90" on a notepad. "You—130 kilometers per hour."

No way, I think to myself. *This is a trap.*

He asks for my license.

"Pay ninety euros now or I keep your license."

His partner chimes in as "the bad cop."

"Pay now, no negotiation."

I am overcome by a whirlwind of emotions.

Shit.

... I know I wasn't going 130. Must have been someone else. Many cars zoomed by and they stopped me?

... Is he even the real cop? Should I ask to see his badge? Real policemen don't ask for money on the spot, right?

... These bullies. They have no proof.

... What? They just walked back to their car (with my license)? Pricks!

... What if we drive away now? I like my license picture though.

I decide that these French policemen are bullies and I won't go down without a fight. And since I am certain of my innocence, I also decide that they're targeting us because we're Chinese. That raises my rage to a new level.

As a Chinese, every time I see my people get mistreated, I think about the Bruce Lee movie *Fist of Fury.* In one scene, members of a Japanese dojo showed up at Bruce Lee's Jingwu school during a funeral, looking for trouble. When Jingwu school students refused to fight them, the Japanese "gifted" them a sign bearing the words "Sick Man of East Asia," an insult against Chinese martial arts and the entire race. Later, Bruce Lee showed up alone at the Japanese dojo to return the gift. He kicked everyone's ass, tore off pieces of the "Sick Man of East Asia" sign, and made them eat it.

Making these French policemen eat their speeding ticket is the least I could do for my people.

Angry as I am, I try to clear my head and think through what I should to do. Nelson Mandela said that if you talk to a man in a language he understands, that goes to his head. If you talk to him in his language, that goes to his heart. My lack of French proficiency precludes me from speaking to their hearts. I am on their turf playing their own game. In the past English Premier League season, home teams enjoyed a 49 percent win rate, versus 29 percent playing away. I don't like my odds winning an argument against them.

So I walk up to their car and start by thanking them for doing their job.

"I'm having a difficult time believing that I was speeding," I add. "It was two-lane bumper-to-bumper traffic for the most part, and I didn't pass one single car."

They were expecting anger, and seem taken aback by my attempt to reason.

"I really think you had the wrong guy. Can your colleague share as to how fast and where I was speeding?"

He mutters something in French to his partner, who shrugs and contacts their other colleague with his walkie-talkie. I smell blood; they are second-guessing themselves. Justin, DJ, and Brian walk over to back me up.

"We're just here for the tournament. We aren't looking for trouble," Justin adds. I hope they haven't seen the news about the English and Russian hooligans.

They call their colleague again, but I can see that the conviction in their tone is slipping away.

"We double-checked with our colleague. It was you he said," the officer says. "But I didn't see with my eyes. This time I make exception. You go now."

We thank him, turn around, and walk back to our car in the slow, measured steps of the righteous.

"How about that?" I mumble.

"Should we do the Ronaldo Super Saiyan celebration now or wait?" Justin smirks. We are still in their full sight.

"You were speeding," Brian says.

"Shut up. You were all snoring in the back."

"There was one stretch you just took off," DJ says.

"No, I didn't," I say. "Did I?"

After the glamour tour of Monaco and Saint-Tropez, Marseille brings us back to the pained reality of real life. We witness a motorcycle accident in which the at-fault cyclist calls up his crew to have the victim surrounded. Later on, we see an angry man tip over several parked motorcycles. He then rips off all his clothes—shirts, shorts and all—like the Hulk. An even more muscular man, whom we initially mistake as the bike owner, tears off his shirt and runs over from across the street.

Are we about to see French Street Fighters?

But the second guy turns out to be an ally trying to keep his friend out of trouble.

"Dude, don't take off your shirt if you aren't gonna fight!" Justin huffs.

In supermarkets, shopping carts have long metal rods welded on for theft prevention—not theft of the merchandise, but the carts themselves. The weld job is crude, done by someone with no regard for aesthetics. It is hard to imagine that Le Club 55 and La Terrasse are only the next city away.

Our Airbnb du jour is an art studio with bedrooms attached on the far end. The concrete floor and open-air Zen garden give the place a unique, futuristic touch. Some would really appreciate its qualities.

Not us.

We prefer traditional comfort—AC, soft beds, TV, and plush towels all day. We are Shangri-La boys.

We barge in through the front door to the welcoming sight of Dave, Kenny, and Sho.

"*Dim-sin!*" Justin yells. *Dim-sin* (點先), not to be mistaken with dim sum (點 心), is the Cantonese equivalent of "what's up."

"Yo!" Kenny fist bumps each of us with a huge smile on his face.

Dave, in his guns-blazing undershirt, comes over and gives Justin a man hug.

"Yo, Brian, I heard you lost all the money," Sho teases. "Told you not to go for England, man."

"Hi, Djibril," I say to our host, shaking his hand. "Thanks for letting us stay here."

Kenny, Dave, and Sho arrived a few hours ago. Their stuff is all over the living room already. The tension in the air suggests they haven't exactly hit it off with Djibril. Banter and hyena giggles take over this tranquil art studio.

"We have neighbors here," Djibril sneers through gritted teeth, gesticulating us to keep it down. His shrine is pillaged before his eyes.

My mom has arrived in Marseille for tomorrow's game. We meet up with her for dinner at Chez Fonfon, a renowned bouillabaisse restaurant in Vallon des Auffes, a little fishing community just outside of Marseille.

"Have you had bouillabaisse before?" my mom asks. "My host said this is the best place for it in Marseille."

"Only about three times in the past week. We even made it ourselves last night," I reply.

There are two parallel conversations at the table. On one end, Justin and the boys lay down the rules for the championship belt.

"Tomorrow afternoon, we are competing in a footgolf tournament. Winner takes the belt. And people can challenge for it for the rest of the trip," Justin shouts.

"I'm going home with the belt at the end of the trip," Dave says. "I call it now."

On the other end, I share with my mother and her

husband Peter the "joy" of traveling with my friends and their Facebook accounts.

"I'm ready to kill them and smash all their phones," I say with a smile, watching Dave and Justin make side bets for their next beer pong match.

Six years ago, armed with only her husband's blind allegiance, my mother moved to rural Italy. The born-and-raised Hong Kong city girl thought she could chase a childhood dream of retiring in Europe. I thought the novelty would wane long before she reached old age. But she carved out an industrious life for herself, managing various projects, making friends, learning to cook, and traveling the world. She's even learned enough Italian to get by, no small feat for someone whose previous Italian vocabulary consisted only of Armani, Gucci, and Prada. Always up for an adventure these days, she didn't think twice when I offered her free tickets to a Euro 2016 game and a three-night stay at an Ibiza villa. When you have spare anything and need someone to make the number, she's the person to call.

We sing Justin "Happy Birthday," eat the cake, and head home ready to rage. We walk through the front door to the surprising sight of Djibril sitting at the dining table. Time stops as we try to figure out what is going on.

"Oh em ... hi Djibril," I stutter.

"Wait, is he staying here tonight?" Justin asks in Cantonese.

"I think so. He mentioned it this afternoon," Kenny whispers.

In funereal silence we gather in the living room not knowing what to do.

"Are we just going to bed then?" Dave mumbles.

It's only ten.

This is not how our first night is supposed to go. Still unclear as to how we ended up in this situation, we start breaking out our toiletries to get ready for bed.

"How will we fall asleep so early?" I ask.

All of a sudden, Djibril packs up his laptop and announces that he's leaving for the night. All of us maintain our poker faces, but in our heads we're all doing the Ronaldo celebration.

"Oh. You sure?" Kenny asks.

Six pairs of eyes beam Kenny the death stare. He is a nice guy programmed to always say the right things. Justin will later body slam him as punishment.

"Don't worry, your place is in good hands. We're going to bed soon," I say, trying to keep a straight face.

"I hope so." He leaves and closes the door behind him. I notice a flicker of melancholy in his eyes as the door slams shut. He should have known better.

We count to twenty before breaking out the Red Solo cups and blasting music.

Let the madness begin.

We sweep through Djibril's art studio like a level-ten typhoon. Seven suitcases lay spread eagle on the living room floor. Bags of potato chips have exploded all over the coffee table. The place reeks of Kronenbourg beer. The couches are stripped down to their bare skeletons, the cushions nowhere to be found. After three hours of beer pong and rough-housing, we've torn apart Djibril's place just as he feared.

We don't know how hot it is until we try to go to bed for real this time.

Six hundred US dollars is a lot to pay for a place without air-conditioning. It was bearable when we were drinking beer, but not bedtime. I begin to open the window but Justin tells me off because of mosquitos.

"DJ, can you sing a song?" Sho yells out from a different room. "Can't sleep."

DJ is the worst singer we know. No one keeps a straight face when he sings. DJ mumbles through words he can't pronounce, and reaches for notes he has no business reaching.

"Ok, what do you want to hear?" DJ says, clearing his throat.

"How about K歌之王 ("King of Karaoke")?"

DJ's voice reverberates within this studio-apartment. I giggle myself to sleep.

11

PASTIS — MARSEILLE

I HAVE A MEMORY LIKE AN ELEPHANT. I REMEMBER EVERY
ELEPHANT I'VE EVER MET. –HERB CAEN

I WAKE up the next morning drenched in sweat and in desperate need to empty my bladder. En route to the bathroom, I hear a small trickle of water from the Zen garden. With half-open eyes, I see the back of Sho standing over Djibril's plants.

"You aren't peeing in the garden, are you?" I ask. My voice comes out groggy.

Sho turns to face me; he looks restless and confused.

"I'm watering his plants," he moans, showing me the red Solo cup in his hand.

Today is a big day—footgolf tournament in the afternoon, and Portugal-Poland in the evening. We spend the morning doing our own things. Kenny stays in to work, as he always does when we travel out of country. He has no boundaries. Justin and Dave are off doing their own things, but won't tell us what. Sho, Brian, DJ, and I decide to walk around Marseille. Sho was Justin's soccer buddy in college. He is a professional architect who competes in many public architecture contests. Several times a year, we are all forced to vote for his designs. He's a diehard Liverpool fan and five-feet-six of mischievous energy.

"We still have three extra tickets even after counting your mom," Sho says.

"Don't worry guys. I got it covered," I say.

When Justin and I were trying to figure out what to do with our extra tickets, I scrolled through my contacts and found my college friend Kathleen. We hadn't talked in years, but I remembered she spends her summers in Nice. I texted her to see if she happened to be in France.

She responded right away. She was indeed in France, and would love to join us for the game. She would bring her mom and her mom's friend, too.

"Gerald, would you paint my face?" she asked.

Done.

So Kathleen and her family is in.

"Hmm...Kathleen from college huh?" Brian shoots me a dirty look.

"No man," I tell him, "she's just a friend."

When we come back from lunch, Justin is already in full soccer gear. Under Armor shirt, compression shorts, hair in the old-school Beckham slick-back look, he looks ready to play in the Champions League final. He is determined to win our footgolf tournament.

"It's like thirty degrees out by the way," I snort.

He ignores my comment. He and Dave are passing a ball back and forth, sweating like they've been warming up for the past hour.

"I'm ready for a nap," Sho says.

First things first—a pre-tournament photoshoot.

With the music on at full blast, we slip into brand-new jerseys custom-made for the occasion. DJ sets up his camera tripod to find the perfect angle for our group photo.

"Kenny, can you open the sliding glass doors? Pull the curtains back to let in more light," DJ orders as he bends down and peers into the eyepiece of his camera. "Actually, not all the way back. Halfway—looks cool with the breeze."

Following DJ's lead, we go through all the permutations— with ball and without; smiling and not smiling; funny and serious. I am exhausted by the time we're done with the photo shoot.

We arrive at Le Golf de Marseille La Salette in the stifling heat. Carrying an absurd amount of gear—cameras, GoPro, beer, and cleats to change into—we are already sweating bullets before tee off.

We move through the first couple holes at a snail's pace, capturing every shot on video. Brian, DJ, Kenny, and Sho are playing for the videos; only Justin and Dave are serious about winning the belt.

"Quiet!" Justin snaps, lining up a putt.

This course is one tricky track. Precision is paramount— landing ten feet off target can set you back as much as eighty yards. This is a true test of course management, creativity, and accuracy. Brian makes a couple of costly mistakes early on and takes himself out of contention. DJ, who was always going to finish last, shifts his focus to photography after blowing up the third hole. Steady Kenny simply lacks the raw power to compete with the big dogs.

I become fidgety by how slowly we are moving. Initially, I have asked our driver to pick us up at 5:30 p.m. By the fourth hole, I text him to push it to 6 p.m. Then to 6:30, and 7:00. By the sixth hole, the driver tells us to forget it.

"Traffic into Marseille will be very bad after seven. Sorry."

There is not a single Uber in the area. I start to panic that we'll miss the Portugal game tonight.

Oh my god. We can't miss the game. We came all the way here for this.

What will my mom and Kathleen do? I have the tickets.

"Let's pick it up guys," I urge, playing a full hole ahead from the pack to set the pace.

"Relax man. Just enjoy," Brian says.

On the tee box of the final hole, realizing how much of a party pooper I've been, I force myself to smile and tally up the score.

"Alright, Justin leads Dave by one going into the final hole. Good luck gentlemen."

Dave misses the fairway and scramble for a par. With a seven-footer for the win, Justin misses. They finish tied for first.

"What? So what do we do now?" Justin asks in panic. He doesn't want to share the belt.

"Sudden death playoff. Let's go!" Dave cries.

"No, no, no. We're late. We're just gonna do matching of cards for tiebreak," I say.

I put their scorecards side by side, comparing their scores hole to hole from last to first.

"Okay, Justin won. Let's go," I announce and shake Justin's hand.

"What the hell, man? That's bullshit!" Dave yells, but I am already gone.

There's only one thing on my mind—find a ride back. I start sprinting in full panic without a clue where the clubhouse is. I find it eventually.

"Two taxis to Marseille, please! Now!" I yell across the Pro Shop, about to pass out from exhaustion.

I lean over the counter panting and watch as the girl makes the phone call. Ten minutes later, the boys sashay their way back to the clubhouse. Their lack of hustle infuriates me; I wait outside in the parking lot while they race each other to uploading footgolf videos on social media. I start breathing again once we're safely in the car back to Marseille. Our driver moves through small streets like 007; it looks like we are going to make the game after all.

"Told you we would make it, bro," Justin says, stroking my back.

I force a smile knowing I probably overreacted.

We change into our Portugal jerseys and head to the stadium. With a ballpoint pen, I write "Nani #17" on the back. Wrapped in a Portuguese flag is DJ, the guy who almost didn't come on the trip because it didn't make economic sense for a non-soccer fan.

"When did you start supporting Portugal?" I ask.

"Always. I'm from Macau. That makes me Portuguese."

He always finds a way to get into the moment. His principles are so haphazard and adaptable that it's hard not to love him.

"Let's go boys! My friend is waiting!" I yell, resuming my role as the nervous timekeeper.

"Gerald, who's your friend?" Sho asks, flashing a mischievous smile. He is single and knows I'm bringing a girl friend.

"Kathleen. My good friend from college."

"That's it? Don't lie man," he flashes an evil grin.

Kathleen has no shortage of admirers. But I never thought about her romantically. College boys are wired to go after girls. By not doing that—sometimes by choice, sometimes the lack thereof—I'm blessed with many good female friends to this day.

We meet up with my mom and Peter at a bar outside the stadium. Kathleen and her family are already there when we arrive.

"Gerald!" she leans in for a hug.

"You guys find parking okay?" I ask, limping in with a half hug knowing how sweaty I must be.

"Guys let's take a shot." Sho hands out seven milky-looking shots that nobody asked for.

"What's this?" Justin spits, wrinkling his nose.

"I don't know. Some French stuff," Sho says. "It's the first item on the menu."

I grip the glass and toss it back like a champion. As one-point-five ounces of potency touch my tongue, a memory train roars to life. It burns loud; it burns clear.

"My god that tastes like shit," Brian yells, his face contorting in pain.

"What's this shit?" Dave asks, scrambling for the menu. "*Pastis?*"

The revolting taste harkens back to 2006 when we tried a cocktail called Machu Picchu and vomited back into the glass. In 2016, pastis, a summer favorite in southern France, has us all scrambling for chasers.

Travel writer Peter Mayle had the following to say about pastis:

> For me, the most powerful ingredient in pastis is not aniseed or alcohol but ambience, and that dictates how and where it should be drunk. I cannot imagine drinking it in a hurry. I cannot imagine drinking it in a pub in Fulham, a bar in New York, or anywhere that requires its customers to wear socks. It wouldn't taste the same. There has to be heat and sunlight and the illusion that the clock has stopped. I have to be in Provence. (Peter Mayle, *Toujours Provence*)

DJ and I first crossed paths with this milky bombshell eight years ago in France. We followed Mayle's exact recipe— Provence, summer sunshine, the outdoors at the port ... the whole nine yards. We tried it both neat and diluted, both to devastating results.

A two-time drinker now—and with the benefit of eight years of maturity—I offer my honest account:

> For me, the most powerful ingredient in pastis is not aniseed or alcohol but the drinkers themselves. I cannot imagine drinking it in a hurry. In fact, I cannot imagine drinking it at all, of my own will. Money has to be involved. I have to be in Provence, already drunk, and on a dare. (Gerald Yeung, *Kong Boys*)

Don't tell me it's an acquired taste.

Stade Vélodrome is the home of Olympique de Marseille. It is the largest soccer stadium in France with a capacity of over sixty-seven thousand. We have three different sets of tickets to the game. Kathleen's mom and her friend are in the third row by the corner flag. Their seats are great for photos, but not so much for following the game. All my friends are on the long side of the stadium behind the dugout. My mom, Peter, Kathleen, and I are on the opposite side next to diehard Polish fans. I send a picture to my brother in London.

"Does Mom know Poland scored already?" he asks. "She usually doesn't know."

He once brought her to White Hart Lane as Tottenham took on Manchester City. Tottenham dismantled the reigning champion in a 4–1 thriller. My mom said she had a grand time and found the game engaging, but when my brother told her the final score, she asked, "When did they score four goals?"

A terrific wing play sets up Bayern Munich's star striker Robert Lewandowski to put Poland ahead after just two minutes. Poland squanders several opportunities to extend the lead and allows Portuguese boy wonder Renato Sanches to pull Portugal level.

Kathleen is a complete novice in soccer but is infinitely curious.

When do you do a throw-in?

Do these teams ever play against Real Madrid? Are they better than Madrid?

What is offside?

Can we take a selfie together? Down there?

As a good ambassador of the game, I'm happy to answer her questions.

"When's the final? If I get a ticket do you think I should go?" she asks.

Every summer, Hong Kong invites big European clubs to play exhibition matches. Many die-hard fans don't get tickets; they all go to sponsors and people with connections. I learned that fandom alone doesn't sustain the sport—money does.

"If you have tickets to the final," I tell Kathleen, "you should go."

She smiles.

The police begin to shore up late in the second half as tension heightens among the fans. There isn't much happening on the field; the fans find their own extracurricular to expend all their pent-up energy. Where Irish fans chose peaceful expression of their passion, some Polish fans here exude a more sinister energy.

The game plays to a 1–1 draw after extra time. Portugal advances after the penalty shootout. Renato Sanches is a box-to-box monster with the makings of a Pogba. He's the real deal.

"Penalty shootouts are so cruel," my mom rues.

Welcome to soccer.

Leaving the stadium, we discuss key moments of the match.

"It was so cool!" Kathleen beams. "Thanks again for inviting!"

"Amazing!" my mom echoes.

Peter yawns and nods in silent agreement. It's well past midnight. I actually found the game quite boring, but they don't need to know. Now that we've fulfilled the lifelong dream of seeing a Euro game in person, I'm happy to follow the rest of the tournament on TV.

Then out of nowhere, something lunges from behind and jostles me off my feet. A hunky Portuguese fan comes flying and looks to be on the run. We turn around and see a mob of angry Polish fans charging at the man. They lift him up by his limbs and throw him onto the ground. It's difficult to see the melee through the dust, but I can hear the *omph, omph* sounds of punches and kicks connecting. This is real street fighter stuff; the Portuguese fan lies defenseless on the ground until several of his compatriots jump in and chase off his assailants. I get a good look at him; he has his ninja turtle build to thank for his life.

My mom is petrified. Her face registers the same expression of horror as the time she watched my then twelve-year-old brother bludgeon a pedestrian to death in *Grand Theft Auto 3*. Kathleen sets her questions aside for the moment and quickens her pace. Even I'm startled into sudden vigilance. I didn't notice till now the build of some of these Polish fans; we're walking among some real-life Rocky Gibraltars from *Toy Story*, many of whom need no second invitation to let off steam. We walk Kathleen to the safety of her family.

"Say hi to your dad and brother for me," I hug her and her mom goodbye.

Next, I drop my mom off at her Airbnb.

"I don't feel comfortable with you walking to the train station alone," my mom moans. "It's so dark here."

"There are so many people on the street. What can possibly happen?" I say, which is funny given what we just witnessed. Deep down, I'm a little apprehensive myself.

"Why didn't your friends wait for you?" my mom asks, her jaws tightened.

"Because," I shake my head and chuckle, "that's not how we roll."

"Okay, be safe. We'll see you in Ibiza in a week?" she says.

"Wait, what Ibiza?"

"You invited us to stay at the villa. Remember?"

It has slipped my mind.

"Virginia and your Goo-ma are very excited about it. Don't make a mess at the place. Make it comfortable for them when they arrive," she says.

I can't think that far ahead. I'll worry about that later.

We hug goodbye and I'm on my way. With my hands in my pockets, I take quick, purposeful steps toward the train station. I make it through a subway ride among all Polish fans without incident. But really, who would have messed with a Portugal fan with a DIY Nani jersey?

Getting off at the Saint-Charles station, I run into the boys. I thought they would have been home long ago.

"Wow, you guys weren't waiting for me, right?" I ask. Maybe this is how we roll after all.

"Nah, we just got here," Sho explains.

"You guys missed some serious UFC action," I say.

With Ronaldo and company taking the game into extra time and penalties, we didn't get home until 2 a.m. An 8 a.m. train to Barcelona awaits us the next morning.

.   .   .

I wake up to my 6:30 alarm. With my bags all packed, I begin to clean the house. I sweep up the chips scattered on the coffee table. I throw out the trash. I recycle beer bottles across the street. I put the dirty glasses in the sink. I reassemble the couch I took apart the other night during my desperate search for a better spot to sleep. I recycle more beer bottles across the street. I stack the beer pong cups. I throw away Kenny's French card game played with a deck of only thirty-two.

At 7 a.m., Djibril lets himself back into the apartment. He catches a lone figure eating cereal in his Zen garden. He waters his plants and inspects every corner of his place for damages. He puts on latex gloves with a loud snap, scoffing at the mess we left in the kitchen in spite of my attempt to clean up. He puffs as he rearranges the couch cushions that I incorrectly assembled. The disdain on his face says he finds us unworthy of his sanctuary. With his thumb and index finger, he holds the corner of a dripping kitchen rag, the one I used to wipe down his dining table. For his future listings, he will surely include a "no beer pong" clause.

"He's trying to get us out of this place as soon as possible," Brian says as he folds up his dirty shirts one by one before placing them into his laundry bag.

We are tired and grimy, having spent another night without AC.

"This feels like going home after camping. Like not showering for two days," Dave says.

12

AUDITION FOR LOVE — BARCELONA

WE CAN'T RUN FROM WHO WE ARE; OUR DESTINY CHOOSES US. –
DAVID LEVIEN

FINDING ACCOMMODATIONS FOR OUR BOYS' trip is a thankless job.

If you spend too much, people complain. If you spend too little, people complain. If the place isn't nice enough, people complain. If the location isn't central enough, people complain. And if the boys trash the place, you take the heat.

We split up the bookings for this trip. I made the reservation for Marseille and Ibiza. Kenny booked Pamplona and Dave Madrid. Barcelona is Sho's job.

"Sho, this place better have AC," Dave says.

We walk out of Barcelona Sants station toward our apartment.

Sho doesn't say a word. He's nervous.

Luckily for him, he didn't go CB on his boys.

Our place is a duplex penthouse decked out with brand-new appliances and furniture. The floor-to-ceiling windows capture a panoramic view of Barcelona. I can picture Christian Grey living here. Most importantly, the AC is on full blast.

Sho flashes an ear-to-ear smile. "I told you, you guys can count on me."

"Hehehehehe!" Dave lets out his signature horse giggle. "Shut up, Sho. You were shitting your pants earlier."

We all have our own beds, except for Justin and Kenny, who'll be sharing the honeymoon suite.

"We can play beer pong here," Kenny says, ducking under the light and imitating a beer pong throw across the kitchen island. This is a man whose thirtieth birthday cake was shaped like a beer pong table.

When Kenny first met Justin in college, he was a textbook goody-two-shoes. His only notable transgression was cursing on the soccer field. Had he made the right friends, he would have become a model husband, father, and member of society by now. Sadly, he met Justin. After twelve years under Justin's wings, Kenny has become a little monster in his own right now, a regular instigator of daredevil deeds—rave parties, ATV escapades, and jungle survival experiences. When we travel, he is Justin's designated roommate—at less than 140 pounds, Kenny makes for a great wrestling partner. He lets Justin abuse his body at will, a small price he pays for a little brotherly affection.

As a lawyer, Kenny's work ethic is impeccable. His Blackberry never leaves him even on vacation. He is every manager's dream. But outside the office, he is tragically forgetful. It is as if his brain switches itself off when it's not billing hours. On our Kenting trip, he arrived at the airport without his passport. He had to change to a later flight for his own birthday trip. And even when he remembers his documents, he has a tendency to lose them. His backpack and suitcase zippers are always open. A real-life Hansel and Gretel.

. . .

Still exhausted from the previous night, we abandon our grandiose plan to tour Barcelona and opt for an afternoon nap instead. When I come to, it is already 5 p.m. Everyone is still asleep; our usual heavy footsteps, banter, and cackles are replaced by a welcome silence and the faint Jay Chou music looping from Justin's room.

I decide to go on a run.

"Anyone wants to jog to Camp Nou?" I ask.

"I'll come," Justin says.

"Me too," Sho echoes.

Sho and Justin both recently recovered from knee surgeries. Those with healthy ACLs are content to stay in bed.

This is my third time in Camp Nou, but I still get the chills just walking through the gates. We stand on the periphery of the empty stadium, humbled by Barcelona's history. Johan Cruyff, Maradona, Ronaldo, Rivaldo, Figo, Ronaldinho, Messi, Neymar all achieved immortality on this famous ground. Camp Nou holds a special place in the hearts of Man U fans, too. On May 26 1999, down 0–1 and staring at a runners-up Champion's League medal, Teddy Sheringham and Olé Gunnar Solskjaer scored dramatic stoppage time goals to complete an unprecedented treble. Our manager Alex Ferguson became Sir Alex the following summer; his boys in red cemented their place in club and soccer folklore. I missed that historic final thanks to a malfunctioning alarm clock, which, ironically enough, was shaped like a soccer ball and rang to the tunes of "Olé, Olé, Olé." I had followed every match of United's improbable march to the treble up till then, sometimes waking up at 3 a.m. on a school night. To this day, I still tell myself that Man U would have lost if I had watched the game.

We enter the fan store at Camp Nou and are greeted by the entire Barcelona squad in mannequins. I can't imagine buying anything here at these prices, especially the jerseys.

"When you have kids, will you buy them real or fake soccer jerseys?" I ask.

"Real, of course!" Justin shrieks. "They'd get made fun of at school. Can't skimp on this kind of stuff."

We have one night in Barcelona; we plan to make it count.

Kenny finds an American bar that has beer pong.

"We can have dinner and watch the Wales-Belgium game," he suggests.

Nainggolan's long-range laser gives Belgium the lead. Ashley Williams equalizes for Wales before halftime off a corner kick. Then, just like the England-Iceland game, Wales shocks their star-studded opponent. First, forward Hal Robson-Kanu pulls off the most unexpected Cruyff turn in the penalty area and scores the go-ahead goal for Wales.

"Who's Robson-Kanu?" Brian asks.

"Who the hell is Robson-Kanu?" Justin echos.

I look him up on Wikipedia. He plays for Reading, a second division team in England. What a goal. What arrogance to pull it off at this stage. Respect.

Wales will face Portugal next.

Sho has a friend joining us from the UK.

"Guys, this is Heather. Treat her like one of the boys," Sho says.

"Shut up, Simon!" she yells, calling Sho by his real name.

Heather is a London-based doctor. She's in Barcelona this week for a medical conference. She looks smart, wholesome, and girl next door, which makes her cursing all the more surprising.

"What did you do in Barcelona?" Sho asks.

"Fxxk all," Heather replies.

She is a doctor you can count on for the truth.

We split up into two teams for beer pong—America versus the UK. DJ (UC Berkeley), Brian (Carnegie Mellon), and I (Cornell) form team America; Justin (London School of Economics), Kenny (also LSE), and Sho (University of Nottingham) represent the UK. Dave (Australia) sits out.

In Hong Kong Rules Beer Pong, the first shot of each round counts double if you hit the front cup. I didn't know that. And so when I take the first shot and airmail the table, DJ shakes his head in a slow, dramatic way.

"If you're not on form, let me throw first," he hisses.

"Yeah DJ! You da man!" Justin yells.

We've been egging DJ on all trip. He thinks he is LeBron James now.

Tonight's main event is Eclipse cocktail lounge on the twenty-sixth floor of W Barcelona. Located on the beachfront of the Barceloneta boardwalk, the hotel is shaped like a sailboat setting off into the Mediterranean Sea.

We walk across W's chic lobby with the swagger of Mick

Jagger. The hostess puts on our VIP wristbands and sends us up to the twenty-sixth floor.

"DJ, what did the hostess say to you just now?" Justin asks.

"She said I look perfect," DJ replies, shrugging his shoulder. Even complete strangers are stroking his ego now.

In the roped-off VIP area, our table is next to a group of American girls.

"We're here to watch the European Cup," DJ yells over the thumping house music.

"Didn't Argentina win?" the girl from Austin, Texas, asks.

"Haha, no. The *European* Cup."

"Didn't Chile lose?"

Welcome to America.

Out to prove that she can hang with the boys, Heather makes friends with everyone in the club and brings them to our table. Even Dave in his prime is no match for Heather's gallantry.

She pats DJ on the back. "Go talk to her, man," she says, pointing at the lone Asian girl in the club.

"Sorry, I'm not interested in Asian girls anymore," he says.

"DJ, who says Asian girls are interested in you?" I reply.

You learn interesting things about your friends eavesdropping on them talking to strangers. When Brian talks to two French girls with an inexplicable beef with America, he decides to reveal his ties to the country.

"Oh, I was born in San Mateo," Brian says.

After twenty-five years of friendship, I find out tonight that Brian was born a twenty-minute drive from my current home.

"But I went to college in Philadelphia," he adds.

"No, you didn't, you liar," I chime in. "You went to school in Pittsburgh."

He whispers in my ears. "Shh. I always just tell people Philadelphia. It's easier. No one outside the US knows Pittsburgh."

I can't disagree. At least Philadelphia has the 76ers. I miss Allen Iverson. *We here talkin' about practice man.*

When Molly went to Hong Kong on her own for the first time, I asked DJ to take her out. She came back with glowing reviews of the man, whom she dubbed the nicest and most sentimental guy ever. He confided in her about his family troubles, which he'd never opened up to us about.

"He said he's working in finance now but one day he wants to work for the World Bank to help the poor. So sweet."

"Get the hell out," I say, making a mental note to confront DJ about it one day. I don't know which is the real DJ—the one we know, or the one he shows the rest of the world?

The club starts to fill up after midnight. We meet Christina and Maxime. They are from Maastricht, a town in southeast Netherlands.

"I've never heard of Maastricht," I say.

"It's a really cozy city with lots of students," Christina continues. "There's a big campus for innovation and research near the city called Chemelot and ..."

"Okay, okay, I believe you.".

She works for BMW in the front office and maintains a food and health blog. She shows me her website; it looks legit.

Dave and I are telling to them about our trip when a tycoon arrives and makes a shameless, audacious move on Maxime.

He leans in to Maxime. "Come with me to my yacht." He points in the direction of the ocean.

He has reserved two tables for himself and half a dozen scantily clad women he brought to the club. His intentions are clear.

Dave and I sit back and watch this unsavory man work. The aloofness with which he flirts with Maxime disgusts me. He was hardly trying. His body language says, *I'm rich; you're stupid if you don't like me.*

"It's insulting for the girls," I tell Dave, getting all righteous about it all of a sudden.

"What're you laughing at? That's you in ten years, mate," Dave laughs.

Dave and I have front-row seats to the little show he puts on for her. First to arrive is the Dom Pérignon train. We're all too familiar with this dance—the Star Wars theme song comes on as waitresses with big smiles march out hoisting bottles of Dom Pérignon Rosé and sparklers. High-rollers may come in different shapes and forms around the world, but when it comes to showing off, they follow the same formula. I hope he feels that was three thousand euros well spent.

The tycoon passes out flutes to everyone save Dave and me. A second Dom Pérignon train follows. A waitress is now permanently stationed by the man's side filling his glass every time he takes a sip. Dave and I make the most logical move in this situation.

"Dave, let's go" I mumble. "Better not mess with this guy."

He nods.

"It's nice meeting you two," I say to Maxime and Christina. "We should head back to our table before your scary friend kills us."

. . .

We lose count of how much champagne we've had. I no longer recognize anyone at our table.

It's time to go.

We exit the club to the fresh Mediterranean breeze outside the W. I look around. Heather, Brian, and Sho look ready for bed. Justin is wrestling Kenny to the ground. Dave is talking to himself, his body swaying back and forth trying to remain upright. DJ is looking into his reflection trying to fix his hair. This is when I realize—I'm not done partying yet. Not even close.

"Who wants to go to Razzmatazz?" I yell.

A hand rises in the air. DJ never lets me down.

We carry on.

DJ and I trade the fancy W cocktail lounge for a mammoth warehouse-turned-disco. There are five different clubs inside Razzmatazz, each with its own floor and music.

"This is the Costco of clubs," I say.

After dancing to thumping house music in the first-floor disco, we find our way to the rooftop for air. Smokers gather here under the neon Razzmatazz sign. We take a seat on cinder blocks and soak it all in—being young in Barcelona in the wee hours of the night. I feel alive and blessed to be sharing this moment with one of my best friends.

"What should we do with these?" DJ fiddles with our drink vouchers. "You still want to drink?"

I check my phone. It's 3:30 a.m.

"Nah," I say.

I'm not tired yet, but it feels like a good time to go home.

We sink into the back seat of a taxi, relishing the instant lower back relief.

"Did I tell you about the girl from a while back? Should I message her?"

Where alcohol turns some people violent, in DJ it unlocks his secrets and insecurity.

"Why would you message her now?" I slur, my eyes closed. "We're in Barcelona."

"Just wondering."

Soon after DJ and this girl met, they started seeing each other fast and furiously. Five dates in ten days—lunch, coffee, dinner, movie, night walk in Stanley, long drives around Hong Kong Island. It felt like the beginning of a serious relationship.

"She was cute, well-mannered, and smart. And I thought we really clicked."

On their tenth date, which marked a month of their meeting, DJ took her to the peak and asked her to be his girlfriend.

"She didn't say yes or no, or needing more time to think about it. She was quiet the rest of the night," DJ says.

The following week, she didn't return his calls or texts. DJ tried everything to reach out. Deep down, he sensed that this was her subtle rejection.

And then one day out of the blue she said, "Okay, now I accept you."

"I couldn't believe it. So the whole time it was a test?" DJ fumes.

This reminds me of Zlatan Ibrahimović's famous quote when Arsène Wenger asked him to try out for Arsenal—"No way, Zlatan doesn't do auditions."

Apparently, neither does DJ.

"I wasn't upset that she made me prove myself. It was more the way she kept me in the dark the whole time and seemed indifferent to what I had to go through."

My gut says there's more to the story. There always is— sometimes DJ leaves out important details even from us. But tonight he needs a friend, not a judge.

DJ broke it off and hasn't talked to her since. I can still sense his resentment. Maybe his LeBron-like behavior is a facade for his broken heart.

"She missed out, man. Let her live with that," I say.

The apartment is pitch dark and quiet. We are the last ones home. I brush my teeth, slip into my pajamas, and crawl into the sofa bed in the living room. I'm about to turn off the light when DJ comes out of his room in only his underwear. I brace for a tackle, but he just snuggles up next to me.

"Yes?" I ask.

He lies face down and plants his head in the pillow.

Don't you have your own bed, I think to myself.

"Fiona invited me to her wedding," he says, his voice muffled by the down pillow.

"Oh," I say, not knowing how else to respond because I forget who Fiona is. "Are you going?"

He lifts his head up, thinks for a moment, and without turning to look at me, he says, "Yeah ..."

Like the other girl, Fiona put DJ through an audition. For six months DJ and Fiona were seeing each other doing things like a real couple. But the whole time DJ never felt she was committed.

"She even called it a 'trial relationship,'" he recounts.

At the end, he was the one who broke it off. She was the

only girl that DJ has ever truly loved. They were never a real couple, even though they loved each other, according to DJ.

"The older we get, the more I regret who I've been in all my failed relationships. Some people figure it out early. I've had to learn the painful way," he sighs.

"Love by trial and error," I tease.

I've had regrettable moments myself. I've only had two serious girlfriends—Molly and my ex-girlfriend Kim. Before them there was a girl I've known for the better part of my life. I was a first-class jerk to her. We went to the same school in Hong Kong. We were mutually interested in each other in spite of our two-year age gap. She got my number through my brother's friend and cold called me at home one night. From there, we spent hours on the phone, which was as close to dating as it could be for a fourteen-year-old boy and twelve-year-old girl in Hong Kong. One day while I was out with Justin, Brian, and the guys, she came over to my house to hang out with my brother and made me my favorite mango desert.

The only problem was my friends.

They teased me about "going out" with a younger girl. Today, I can appreciate her qualities, but back then, my guy friends were my world.

One day, a typhoon hit and school was canceled. I had my friends over and they wanted to prank call her. I wasn't keen on the idea, but relented to peer pressure. I pretended to be the admission officer for the US boarding school her older brother was applying to and asked her a bunch of questions about her brother, all while my friends were listening on speaker phone. She knew it was me, and even ask "are you Gerald Yeung" at one point. But she played along. Afterward, she called me and asked me about it, which I denied.

Then, before I left Hong Kong for boarding school, she came to my classroom one recess and slipped me a note. My friend Stephen got ahold of it before I had a chance to read it, and instead of fighting him to get it back, I acted like I didn't care as he read the heartfelt letter aloud to the entire class. She left for boarding school herself two years later. We kept loosely in touch through high school and college, but only on my terms and when I felt like it. She should have stayed away.

My junior year in college, I asked her to come to my fraternity's Homecoming weekend. She rode the bus for four hours from New York City to Ithaca. I enjoyed her company, but I didn't really pay her the attention she deserved.

"Have you ever liked me?" she asked me.

I stared at my computer screen pretending to be doing homework. I didn't answer. She took the bus back to the city soon after.

I couldn't answer that question then; I can't answer that question now. Our relationship was never about her and me. I made every decision based on what my friends would think. I never asked myself what I wanted. I thought being older gave me the right to treat her the way I did. It was wrong.

Today she's an independent woman with her own global business. If Facebook pictures say anything, she looks happily married and living a fabulous life. I am happy for her. And if she ever reads this: I am sorry.

13

LONG ISLAND ICED TEA — IBIZA

SOMETIMES LIFE HITS YOU IN THE HEAD WITH A BRICK. DON'T
LOSE FAITH. –STEVE JOBS

HOW TO BE "DA MAN"?

In our early twenties, "da man" was the one who drank the most, which was between Lulu and Justin. At twenty-five, "da man" was the biggest badass, the rule breaker. Justin was the frontrunner again. Now into our thirties, if you stay up past 3 a.m, you're "da man." I have always been a bottom feeder in all three age groups. But last night, I was "da man."

When Chinese melodies start flowing through the apartment, I know Justin is up.

Brian steps into the living room with heavy circles under his eyes.

"Kenny and I are officially off Dave duty for the rest of the trip," he announces.

After DJ and I had left for Razzmatazz, Snake and Kenny were left to wrangle Dave into submission. The Barceloneta boardwalk was not exactly a taxi haven at that hour, so they waved down a rickshaw.

"Sants station? Fifty euros," Juan the rickshaw driver said.

They did a double take.

"You sure? It's pretty far," Brian said.

"We can take turns pedaling," Kenny proposed.

"No, no. I pedal okay."

Brian, Kenny, and Dave jammed into the carriage; Juan pedaled away.

The hotel was at least an hour away by rickshaw, and the roads of Barcelona traverse some tricky slopes.

"Sorry. I can't no more," Juan huffed. "You take taxi here okay?"

Kenny and Brian thanked him for his effort. Juan dropped them off in a busier area, but Spanish taxi drivers wanted nowhere near Dave.

"He had this giant wet spot on his jeans," Brian explains.

"So what did you guys do?" Justin asks, sitting on the foot of my sofa bed in a neon yellow T-shirt.

"We wandered on the street for ages. Then we finally found a taxi driver willing to take us home," Kenny moans.

Horse giggles emerge from Dave's room. If he feels any remorse at all for Brian's troubles, it doesn't show.

We didn't know Dave from school. Justin met him at a club one night and, for the price of two Long Island iced teas, recruited him onto his soccer team.

Dave goes by many names. Dave, Master Tse, and Mr. Perfect. We all hit it off with him from the get-go. He's a great wingman and an endearing silly drunk. We embrace him even though girls gravitate toward him. He and Justin are the undoubted alphas of the group. They have a special bond where they stroke each other's egos. Dave is a shameless narcissist. Once, we had to come up with a last-place punishment for our fantasy soccer league.

"Let's do an embarrassing photoshoot," I suggested. It was

a popular thing to do in America. Losers in fantasy sports had to shoot an entire calendar of photos in compromising poses.

"It won't work," Sho said. "Dave will lose on purpose."

Justin has Spiderman's sense of direction. During our run to Camp Nou yesterday, we passed a Japanese restaurant along way.

"Let's come here for lunch tomorrow," Justin suggested. "Kenny is gonna be so happy; he loves dragon rolls."

We didn't write down the address or make an effort to remember the surroundings. When it comes time to find the place again, I struggle. I try to replay every scene.

"Remember we were making fun of Ken's mannerisms yesterday at the park?" I ask Justin and Sho. "Was it before or after the restaurant?"

Did we make the turn one block or two after Domino's? Did we pass a supermarket? The only thing I remember is zigzagging through the small streets for over two miles.

Thankfully, we have Justin.

"Dude, did you black out?" he looks at me like I'm playing. "It's simple. We made a turn here at this tapas bar. You recognize the pharmacy sign, right? Then we'll see a park with all those ping pong tables. We even joked that if Kenny were here he would make us play beer pong right there and then. This was where we started making fun of Kenny for always saying, "yes, yes." Then you just cut diagonally across the park and it should be coming right up. Oh and there was a pharmacy right across the street. Can't miss that. Actually, I think that's it right there," he points.

Lo and behold, there it is. Kenny can now have his dragon rolls.

We march into an empty restaurant, interrupting their staff lunch.

"Oh, please come in!" the owner says with a big smile, rising to his feet to turn on the AC.

They bring us hot teas and menus. This is a Chinese-owned Japanese restaurant, which normally wouldn't be our first choice, but it's still good to see fellow countrymen.

"Where are you from?" the lady asks in Mandarin. She seems to be the *lo-ban-leung* (老板娘), the Cantonese term for "owner's wife."

We tell her Hong Kong.

"*Ngo dei wu nan yun,*" she says in labored Cantonese, telling us they are from Hunan Province.

We laugh, appreciative of her effort.

"You look like a Hong Kong celebrity," she says pointing at Justin and then to Kenny. "And you too."

Justin we know. He looks like Jackie Cheung, a Hong Kong singer so legendary that his popularity spans both our parents' and our generation. We call him *gall-sun*—God of singing.

But Kenny?!

"Yeah, he does," Justin quips, "Jasper Tsang."

Mr. Tsang is the President of the Legislative Council of Hong Kong, known more for his political acumen than his looks.

"To Jasper," Kenny raises his glass.

Next stop—Ibiza.

. . .

Our flight to Ibiza is delayed several hours. Sho and Kenny have an idea to kill time.

"Check out this video," they say, looking up to no good.

We huddle around Kenny's phone.

"Hehehehehe, let's do it," Dave horse giggles.

Brian and DJ want in too.

"I'm not doing it," I blurt, "I'll film y'all."

"No, you're doing it. I'm filming," Kenny insists.

We sit down in crew formation on a moving walkway and row an imaginary boat. Onlookers laugh and even take videos of our "race." But the real race, it turns out, happens after when they all try to be the first to upload the video on Instagram.

At long last, we are ready for boarding. Heading to our gate, Sho raises his phone in the air, prompting everyone to assume group selfie position behind him. Not a stride broken. Not one word exchanged. We are like a well-oiled selfie machine.

"Henrikh Mkhitaryan to Man U. Thirty million pounds. They just confirmed," Kenny announces.

"Who's that?" Justin asks.

"He plays for Dortmund I think. Attacking midfielder," I say.

"Is he good?" Justin asks.

"With a name like this, he better be," I reply.

"Check out the private jets," DJ cries as our plane taxis in the Ibiza airport.

"Which one is Rooney's?" Brian asks. Rumor has it that he's in Ibiza with family after England's Euro 2016 exit.

What does the European party capital look like? Are we going to see stars everywhere? We can't wait to find out.

Our villa is only half a mile from the airport. The bus drops us off roadside next to a block of warehouses. This feels more like Kwai Tsing Container Terminals in Hong Kong than a resort neighborhood. As the person who booked the place, I am sweating now.

"Now you know how I felt yesterday," Sho whispers in my ear.

Ibiza is *the* main event of our trip. The expectation for this villa is sky-high. Justin confided in me that whenever he was sad in the last few months, he opened the link to this villa to cheer himself up.

"It kept me going through the hard months in school," he said.

No pressure there.

If this place flops, my friends won't give me grief, at least right away. My family won't complain, at least not to me. But I would never forgive myself for letting so many people down.

I run a full block ahead of everyone, one hand gripping my phone on GPS, one hand rolling my suitcase.

Only two hundred yards from the place. I follow the directions and turn into a side street.

I pray that a change of scenery will be imminent and dramatic. Cold sweat pools at the base of my neck.

And then, I have arrived.

"I think this is it," I motion, standing in front of a gated property behind tall privacy walls. I jump to try to peer over the walls but I can't see anything.

Others have caught up. The earlier chatter is gone. The silence is deafening as we brace for a miracle.

"The instructions say to look for the gate remote ..." I am trying to read off my phone but DJ already pushes the gate open.

We crane our necks for the big reveal.

Here we go.

A chalk white villa stands at the end of a long driveway, the kind of house I picture a drug lord would call home. Through a pair of floor-to-ceiling glass doors, the living room opens to a backyard straight from the magazines. Swaying palm trees flank both sides of a resort-grade swimming pool, daring us to jump in. We scamper into the house and run wild from room to room. On the second-floor mezzanine, three suites overlook the living room and the backyard. This place is made for a boys' getaway. I breathe a sigh of relief.

"Woot woot!" Dave yells.

"Hey guys, don't completely tear the place up," I warn, already looking ahead to the next problem.

"What's the Wi-Fi?" DJ with his customary question.

Sho tosses his cap from the mezzanine down to the living room. Let the party begin.

I read through the information binder that comes with the house as Brian puts on the quarter-final game on TV.

"Woah, you can order pizza delivery on WhatsApp in Ibiza," I say.

Live and learn, America.

Giant slayer Italy is taking on world champion Germany at Stade Matmut Atlantique in Bordeaux. Midway through the second half, Germany finally breaks down the staunch Italian defense. But Bonucci's penalty kick equalizes for Italy in the seventy-eighth minute after Boateng's inexplicable handball.

At 1-1, the game returns to a defensive stalemate; it will be another penalty shootout. Both teams produce some of the worst penalties ever seen at this level. Chief among all is Simone Zaza, who was brought on at the death of extra time presumably for his penalty expertise. He steps up to the ball with a bizarre run up and blasts it into the stratosphere. The Internet will have a field day for weeks to come. Neither side seems keen on winning the game. In the end, Germany, the taller of two dwarves, advances to the semis.

"This is like the South Park episode on Little League Baseball when both teams were trying to lose," I say.

No one knows what I'm talking about because they don't watch that stuff in Hong Kong.

"Alright, what's the plan for tonight?" Kenny asks.

My share of planning ended with this villa. From here on, it's all play for me.

"We didn't book anything," Justin explains. "Let's head to Playa d'en Bossa and see where the night takes us."

The Ibiza in my mind has always been a wild, free-flowing Dom P party paradise for the rich. But the scene at Playa d'en Bossa feels more like late night Bangkok than Monte-Carlo. It's only 11 p.m., but this place already has a sloppy drunk quality to it. Tourists fisting oversized sugary cocktails shuttle in and out of cheap motels. Sunburnt teenagers linger about on the street, not ready to go to bed. Cheap party accessories are sold everywhere.

I can't picture George Clooney hanging with this crowd.

We kick off on draught beers at Zanzibar and make our way to Dunes. We look far from our best. Snakey nurses his drink and seems ready for bed. Sho's glass is left untouched. Dave is so quiet that no one notices he's even there. Kenny has his glasses and cardigan on; he makes an early exit. Staying up for consecutive nights is consigned to memories of wilder days.

"Let's go to Pacha," DJ pleads. "Paris Hilton is DJ-ing."

Pacha is on the other side of the island. It seems a tall order. And at 1 a.m. already, is it really worth it?

"What time do the clubs close?" we ask the bartender at Dunes.

She smiles. "8 a.m."

"Oh, never mind."

We all look at each other, waiting for someone else to decide. Moments like this call for a leader.

I grab Sho's Long Lun and chug it.

"Alright boys, let's go to Pacha!" I call.

We belt out *Heroes* on the taxi over.

Rum was once part of the British Navy's ration. Sailors used to test the quality of their booze by mixing it with gunpowder and lighting it. If the mixture ignited, it was good rum. By this logic, the British Navy would drink the remnants of my stomach the morning after Pacha.

I don't regret going to Pacha. I had one drink with the boys at the bar and got jostled around on a jam-packed dance floor. My next memory was hugging the toilet bowl until I fell asleep.

"Um ... DJ, what happened to Paris Hilton?" I ask, staggering out to the living room in pain. I was lied to about Paris Hilton. Either DJ got the date wrong or we just missed her.

"Gerald you look like shit," Brian says.

"Yeah, I don't feel great." I explain.

Kenny holds out for a fist bump. "Weak sauce, bro."

"Sorry Kenny, only people who made it to Pacha, please," I say.

We've made a mess of the house after just twelve hours. In my hungover stupor, I clean up the pizza boxes and try to put the place back in reasonable shape.

DJ and Sho are lounging poolside under the scorching sun. I cringe as I know for sure they don't have on any sunblock.

We need to shop for groceries this morning. At 11 a.m., everyone is still lounging about on their phones. The old Gerald would have looked up the supermarket address, called a cab, and gotten everyone out the door.

But that Gerald is dead. The new Gerald isn't going to plan the whole day while his friends Instagram, play beer pong, and fix their hair.

Around noon, Justin starts to rally the troops. You can hear his stomach growl.

"Hey Gerald, have you called a taxi?" he asks.

"Nope." I play with my phone on the sofa without looking up.

If he senses something is off, he doesn't call me out on it.

Grocery shopping for seven men feels like preparing for the apocalypse—toilet paper, shower gel, a crazy amount of food, and even water. Many gallons of water.

"Why do we need twenty gallons of water?" I question.

"Drinking and cooking," Justin replies. "The tap water tastes strange. I won't even boil noodles with it."

People in line behind us give us dirty looks when they see our four carts of food and supplies.

Taxis are hard to come by here, so DJ and I start looking while the others queue up to check out. After fifteen minutes, I finally wave one down.

"Can you wait a few minutes?" I plead.

"But I turn on meter, okay?"

I nod.

I run inside and tell the boys to hurry. With the meter running, Dave does curls with water jugs outside the supermarket as Kenny takes a video. I am about to lose my shit.

I send the boys on their way while DJ and I wait for another taxi.

"Did you ask the taxi driver to call another taxi?" he asks.

"Nope" I say, daring him to ask me why.

I'm tired of taking care of things. Probably sensing something is off, DJ doesn't press on. We ride back to the house in silence.

Back at the house, Justin, Sho and I make lunch. Justin makes a mean scrambled eggs that would make Johnny Drama proud. Sho, the microwave cuisine specialist, serves up instant macaroni and cheese. All the food vanishes within minutes. I marinate chicken wings and steak for dinner barbecue.

"My friend is in Ibiza too and said he saw LeBron, CP3, and D Wade yesterday," Brian tells us over lunch.

I make everyone put away the dishes the moment we finish eating.

"What should we do this afternoon?" Sho asks.

"Gerald, did you bring the beer pong floatie?" Kenny asks.

I nod. I've been carrying it all around Europe waiting for this moment.

"Pool beer pong this afternoon for the championship belt!" Justin announces.

For this trip, I commissioned a custom-made leather championship belt, engraved with our seven initials, the start and end dates of our trip in Roman numerals, and every city on our itinerary. In the big center plate, I "borrowed" Johnny Drama artwork with the words "Entourage Season Finale" underneath. I even emailed HBO about copyright and proceeded when I didn't hear from them after weeks.

Against all odds, Kenny beats DJ in the final for the championship. In a teary post-match interview, Kenny dedicates his victory to Brian's mom.

"This win validates every decision I've made in my life."

The conviction in his voice feels almost foreign to his usual submissive demeanor. In one fell swoop, all is redeemed. The corporate slave and Justin's boy toy is reborn as our beer pong champion.

With the title belt decided, we break off for our own activities. I lounge by the pool and listen to Justin Bieber's "Love Yourself" on repeat, a song about moving on from a selfish, narcissistic girlfriend. Molly calls me on FaceTime to talk about Lupe and other things.

"What did you guys do today?"

"Not much. Grocery shopping, cooking, and a beer pong tournament."

"Really?" she says in feign surprise. "Aren't you guys bored of that game?"

I am a little bit. We don't have a beer pong addiction; we have a competition addiction.

When I hang up, my lounge chair is no longer in the sun. Time to start the grill. DJ offers to help.

"Dude, you are wiping down the grill with this much paper towel?" I bark.

He waves the greasy paper towel in my face. "Do you want to eat this?"

While we are arguing, the wind blows the entire roll into the swimming pool. There is a saying in Chinese, 亡羊補牢. When a sheep escapes, repair the fence first to stop the bleeding. By arguing with DJ over a few sheets, we lost the whole roll.

I've always cared deeply for our planet. My obsession with living an environmentally responsible life has only deepened through the recent drought in California. These days, a small act of wastefulness is enough to set me off. I was enraged when Lupe chewed up rolls of toilet paper. I remember on one trip with the boys, someone came back late from a club and went straight into the bathroom with a friend. He turned on the shower and let it run for forty-five minutes to drown out his noises. I couldn't fall back asleep, not because of his escapade in the bathroom, but because of all the water he'd wasted.

Tonight I'm making flank steak and Pepsi chicken wings. The wings have been marinating all afternoon and I can't wait to one-up Mr. Boarding School Chef.

"Shit, we're out of charcoal," DJ says, emptying the last of the bag over a dying flame.

"Are you kidding me?"

The store is fifteen minutes away, so we improvise. I take the steak inside and cook it in the oven. DJ collects fallen leaves and branches from the yard to finish cooking the wings and corn already on the grill.

"Perhaps this adds a smoky flavor to my Pepsi chicken wings," I console myself.

The wings come out a little bland, which is shocking considering the time they spent in my soy-sauce-Pepsi brine. I scan the table for people's reactions. No one finds my wings repulsive, but they aren't raving about them either. I have planned my own parody of Justin's boarding-school-chef-cooking-for-my-boys spiel, but the lukewarm reception forces me to abandon my plan.

After dinner, we are ready to drink again.

"Kenny, I'm coming after your belt, mate," Dave declares.

Flip cup is usually not my game because it makes a big mess, but somehow I get on a run and seize the belt from Kenny.

"Alright, let's go out," I say, trying the belt on for size.

"Hell no, sit back down. We're challenging for your belt right now," Dave orders.

I fend off four title challenges—beer pong, chug off, flip cup—giving definitive proof that drinking games were invented in America. We demolish two bottles of Bacardi Margarita mix in the process and are well buzzed for the Neon Paint party.

I thought that winning the belt would put me in party mood. But stepping into this deserted club to kids half my age, I feel the exact opposite of excitement. It makes sense—most people our age don't like getting their clothes dirty, which is the premise of a Neon Paint party. I wander about by myself spying on my friends. Justin and Dave are halfway to obliteration. Brian and Kenny are talking to random people. Sho operates as a Lone Ranger; DJ stands on the dance floor by himself acting cool. None of us can get it going.

When two ladies in bikinis step onto the raised platform wielding double super soakers, I dart off the dance floor and hide behind the clear plastic curtains.

"No thank you," I object, clearly not living into the spirit of the Neon Paint party.

I watch as these kids get soaked by bright yellow paint from above, wondering how many of them will go to bed that night without showering.

At least I made it to the dance floor. Justin and Brian have fallen asleep in the club foyer. It's time to go home.

But first, Kenny wants food at the Subway next door.

"Hi. Meatball sandwich please," Kenny says to the young sandwich artist.

"Sorry. Your friend has to leave first," she insists, pointing at a lifeless Justin flopped against the wall. A blacked-out Justin weighs about two thousand pounds.

Meanwhile, we hear shouting from outside the restaurant. Brian and DJ are going at each other.

"You were sleeping the whole time!" DJ scoffs. When an evening doesn't pan out, DJ can be quick to point fingers. He feels Brian's lack of energy is to be blamed.

"Yeah? You guys did a lot. You guys rock," Brian yells.

Brian rarely gets so spiteful. Dave pulls them apart before the argument turns physical.

"I want to punch DJ in the face," Brian groans as I drag him away.

When Dj is unhappy, he doesn't hold back.

"It's like operating a space shuttle," he once explained to me, "I like telling the other person the truth, like if you suck at steering the ship, or if the other person is good at shooting down aliens. You need to be open to be an effective team."

Clearly, DJ is not happy with the way Brian was shooting aliens tonight.

We left the villa for the Neon Paint party in clean white shirts. We return to the villa from the Neon Paint party in clean white shirts; this sums up our evening.

Back in the villa, I brush my teeth and change into my pajamas. Before bed, I make one last trip to the living room and see what everyone is up to. Dave is on the couch eating potato chips. Sho and DJ are playing one-on-one beer pong. Kenny and Brian are making instant noodles in the kitchen. Justin is trying to provoke Kenny into a wrestling match, but Kenny keeps his head down and focuses on his noodles. At last, Justin passes out outside on DJ's pizza floaty. Lying with all the grace of a beached whale, he is fortunate that Ibiza is dry and relatively mosquito-free.

GERALD'S PEPSI CHICKEN WINGS RECIPE

1. Crack open a beer for side drinking; this has nothing to do with the recipe
2. Prepare a brine with Pepsi, soy sauce, and a small quantity of vinegar
3. Add garlic powder, black pepper, chili flakes, and whatever spices you find in the kitchen
4. Marinate the wings in the brine for as long as possible
5. Cook them on the grill until they look cooked
6. If you run out of propane or charcoal, find anything burnable to keep the flame going

14

SUSHI POWER — IBIZA

LEAD US NOT INTO TEMPTATION. JUST TELL US WHERE IT IS;
WE'LL FIND IT. –SAM LEVENSON

I GET a text from my mom.

Good morning. Slept well? Don't forget your aunt arrives tomorrow night. Clean up the house and make it nice for her.

How am I going to clean this up? I don't have the energy to start now. And the boys will undo my work tonight anyway. This is a problem for tomorrow.

Crippled by a killer sore throat, I heat up a glass of water and choke down Justin's Chinese herbal medicine. I would do anything to not get sick now.

Two more nights left in Ibiza; five more for the trip.

Finish strong, I tell myself.

I am the last to wake up. In the living room, everyone looks the worse for wear.

"We were too *lawng*, man," Brian concludes, his eyes red and puffy.

"Who's your friend, Sho?" Kenny asks, scrolling through the pictures from the Neon Paint party. She has look Spanish but speaks British English.

"I don't know, but she's half Chinese."

"No way," we laugh.

"I know! But she is. She even showed me her ID. Her last name is Chan. Haha."

"Haha, no way." Somehow we find that hilarious.

Today is Lulu's thirtieth birthday.

"No birthday messages for Lulu," I order, still livid about his betrayal.

"Let's celebrate Brian's birthday instead today," Kenny suggests.

"But it's not for another two weeks," Brian objects.

"Who cares. Happy birthday, Brian," I say.

We shoot the breeze and lose track of time. We would have stayed on that couch for hours if Kenny hadn't reminded us that we had tickets to a beach party starting at noon.

"Day party!?" I ask, petrified by the prospect that it's already 12:08.

"We have to get in by four to keep our table. Let's try to leave by 3:30."

The idea of drinking again in a couple hours has the appeal of a colonoscopy. Justin plunges into the pool to wake himself up.

We go back to our rooms to rest. Dave and Sho read soccer news. DJ plays with his camera. Brian takes a nap. Kenny browses Instagram. Justin listens to Jay Chou. I try to write and take a nap. Three hours to get back in party shape.

Time means different things to different people. When the

clock strikes 3:30, some are at the door ready to go. Some start fixing their hair. Some are just jumping in the shower.

Before we leave for Ocean Beach Club, I sneak into the kitchen for another dose of herbal medicine. Kenny and Justin are already there, looking just slightly less impaired than me.

"Coming in to *pak-yea* too?" Justin laughs. *Pak-yea* 啪嘢 is Cantonese slang for doing drugs.

Doping is more rampant in this kitchen than in the US Postal Cycling Team hotel room. Day drinking requires a different kind of endurance—you don't get to snooze off for the second wind. Sun protection also becomes a factor. Nocturnal animals like us can use every bit of help.

"You really want to get better?" Justin asks, seemingly questioning my resolve.

I nod.

Justin slips me a small packet. It looks like the flavoring packet that comes with ramen noodles. All the words are in Japanese.

"This is the real shit."

What price wouldn't I pay to get well now?

"Bring it."

"Oh, that stuff," Brian interjects. "Have a whole box at home. Don't know the name. It tastes awful."

They're being melodramatic, I tell myself.

I heat up a glass of water.

Justin shakes his head. "Too much water."

I pour some out.

"Less. Trust me, you just want to get it over with."

I tear open the packet and empty it into my glass. The bright yellow powder suspends in the hot water like a snow globe. I stir and watch the liquid turn yellowish brown. I take a sip.

Justin watches as my expression turns from curiosity to anguish.

It tastes like half-dissolved sulfuric chalk, but I still think pastis tastes worse.

"Haha, it tastes like shit right? The people who made it didn't add any flavor whatsoever."

I soldier through it. I'm ready to go home this weekend. To be honest I'm ready to go home now.

We make the trek to the other end of the island again. Another bout of drinking awaits. The hostesses, who look straight out of a Victoria Secret catalog, do their best to make us feel unwelcome. With complete disinterest, they wrap VIP ribbons on our wrists without even making eye contact. Instead, they chitchat among themselves in Spanish as if we don't exist. You know you're getting old when this kind of thing gets to you.

The party is in full swing. It takes us five minutes to nego-tiate the pulsating mass of bodies to our VIP pool bed. This isn't our first beach party, but this place is on a whole different level. On a normal day, Dave's and DJ's shirt would be off by now, but today even they are reserved. The male clientele here appears to be the three hundred Spartans. The servers are all tens, male and female alike. We are usually pretty delusional about our own attractiveness, but even we know we're punching above our weight here. We move about our pool bed tentatively, reconsidering our place in the world.

No one is mocking us at Ocean Beach, but we suspect they are all laughing on the inside. Even Dave is soft-spoken now.

"They probably think we're a bunch of losers," Dave murmurs.

We can use any encouragement now in this identity crisis.

"Don't worry guys. I know a lot of white boys. The more jacked they get, the more insecure they are."

"Really? Is that true?" Dave asks.

I think for a moment. "Hmmm ... mostly true."

Sho bursts out laughing. "Does that mean Dave is insecure?"

Dave worships his body like Scrooge McDuck worships gold coins.

"Eat shit, Sho," Dave rebukes, his shirt still on.

"See that guy over there who keeps flexing his arms and telling everyone he works in finance? Insecurity," I say, sipping a strawberry daiquiri that costs HK$4,000 a pitcher. "And that guy over there with all those tattoos and no neck? Insecurity."

Many Asian boys find white girls intimidating. I used to think the food chain of attraction worked like a pyramid. Caucasians form the top of the triangle, with the French at the very tip. The pecking order in the middle is debatable, but few would disagree that Asians are somewhere at the bottom. After all, video games, ping pong, and math aren't quite most people's idea of sex appeal. It isn't always a bad thing though. Where some girls date French boys for the idea of having a French boyfriend, Molly, who is white, probably loves me for who I am.

As a group, we've had bad outings, but they usually took place at night in relative anonymity; the humiliation felt somewhat private. Here in Ocean Beach under the Ibiza sun, our inadequacy is for the world to see.

"Screw this," Justin snaps, waving the server over. "We're not going down like this!"

Oh no, our eyes widen. *Justin is going for the Dom Pérignon train!* We look at each other. *Who will stop him?*

We all do.

"Don't do it man!" Dave cries.

"It's okay, bro. We'll come around. Don't do this; there's no turning back," Kenny consoles.

"Hey we still have plenty of alcohol. Here, have a beer." I twist open a Bud Light Aluminum.

"Don't be the Dom P guy!" Sho echoes.

"We aren't splitting it," Brian says, pragmatic as always.

Justin smiles.

"Who says I'm ordering Dom P?"

What happens next no one could have predicted. While the wannabes of the world are still obsessing over Dom P, Justin has quietly taken it to the next level. Here in our most desperate moment, he debuts an idea that will change the clubbing game forever.

A jumbo sushi platter.

As if being the only Asian people here is not enough, we double down by ordering the most stereotypical Asian food.

But strangely enough, it works.

When the platter is brought to our table, the whole place gasps. We turn some serious heads. The rugby table next to ours comes over and suddenly wants to chitchat. Slowly, the invisible wall between our table and the rest of the party dissolves.

The sushi, by the way, is delicious.

Our server, Vincent, is a good-humored Belgian pretty boy. He has the Chinese characters Dragon, Love, and Scorpion tattooed on his arm—your typical *gwei-lo* tattoo. He has the self-awareness of knowing how stupid his tattoos look to native Chinese, but he still talks about them openly. The first two characters carry deep meaning for him, he explains, something about his ancestry and motto of life.

"The last one..." he continues, pivoting his palm to make the "more or less" hand gesture.

Was it a buy-two-get-one-free deal? But, respect for being man enough to make light of it.

Vincent tells us about Ocean Beach's best-kept secrets.

While celebrity at an Ibiza beach club is to be expected, some high-profile guests arrive amid more controversial circumstances. Vincent says England Internationals Dele Alli and Eric Dier were among recent customers at Ocean Beach. After a successful season with the Spurs and breaking into the England national team, a vacation was well deserved. The timing, though, is interesting given the entire nation is still fuming over their loss to Iceland. They either don't care, or are oblivious.

"What idiots," Dave says. He has quietly removed his shirt.

Justin has taken a liking to a different server who looks like a cross between David Beckham and Olivier Giroud.

"I want to take a picture with him," Justin gushes.

Dave scoffs. "I bet you his eyes are tiny. Once he takes off his Ray-Bans, he drops to a five."

Meanwhile, someone orders a champagne train.

"Oh, here we go." Brian points to the table behind us.

Five female models catwalk across the club holding big signs that spell "H-A-R-R-Y." Harry is wearing a flat bill hat and a neon green undershirt that accentuates his perfect "Dad bod." He poses for picture with the girls. He doesn't seem like a bad guy—a little dorky— but he looks out of place among his entourage of frat boys.

"Dude, this guy, hahaha," Justin lets out a bellow of laughter, the kind cool kids reserve for making fun of their dorky classmates. "Let me guess who's settling the bill at that table."

Kenny, cackling, extends for a fist bump.

"Justin, what're you laughing at, mate?" Dave says. "He's you in our group—the *Fu-yee-doy* who pays for everything just to hang out with the cool kids."

Justin frowns, not happy with that comment.

Headliner Lovely Laura descends from a globe in an emphatic saxophone performance. Yes—they put her in a globe and drop her from a crane. A sax solo is a rare choice for clubbing music, but she lifts the atmosphere to new heights. Even our table is jolted to some kind of life. I start to wiggle in my Asian boy dance, completely out of rhythm; DJ bobs his head to the beat.

After Lovely Laura bows out to a standing ovation, our drought continues. This is uncharted water for us. Passersby are giving us commiserating looks. Our sushi power has worn off. Justin is out of ideas. Even a Dom P train is unlikely to save us. Dave has slipped his shirt back on again. It's a measure of our ineptitude that the club sends their staff to keep us company, free of charge.

"Whoa, it has come down to this for us, guys." I shake my head in disbelief.

Pity affection usually has no place in our dictionary, but we accept the charity nonetheless. It gives us the much-needed momentum. This and the fact that everyone else in the club has run out of alcohol. We are the booze kingpin now.

The rugby team has fully migrated to our table. Dave, shirt off again, challenges them in arm wrestling.

"Dave! Dave! Dave! Dave!" we cheer. He falls after putting up a good fight.

"Rematch! I'm not done yet. Let's do a scrum!" Dave shouts. A scrum is where rugby players interlock their arms and put their heads down in a formation to push against the opposing team in the same position.

Three of them against six of us. I am sitting this one out; huddling up on a slippery poolside with nine drunk men is a recipe for disaster. I sip a Corona as they line up. All eyes in the club are on us now.

"Three ... two ... one ... Go!"

I cringe as the two sides collide at the edge of the pool. The senseless cheers from the crowd, the low grunts of the participants, and the thumping bass in the background set the perfect stage for a party disaster. Somebody will get hurt. The scrum is hardly moving, but Dave's face says he is pushing at full strength.

"Push! Push!" Dave yells, his face the color of a tomato.

After a respectable ten seconds of stalemate, our rugby friends crumble to an exaggerated fall.

Hong Kong wins.

"Yeah! We did it!" Kenny screams, arms raised and blood dripping out of his nose. Not even a bloody nose can diminish the romance of our triumph.

"Thanks for letting us win," I mumble to one of the rugby guys, offering a reconciliatory handshake.

If there is any doubt that ours was a gifted victory, it is put to rest when one of them lifts Dave up by under his armpits like a baby.

We ride this positive momentum and take over the party. A group of English girls on a bachelorette trip swing by our table. They look to be in their late thirties but still love a party.

"Yeah, I just went through an ugly divorce," Elizabeth exhales. "I'm here to be with the girls and have a good time."

"To letting go." I raise my glass.

We also befriend a trio of Scottish girls—Claire, Eva, and Abbey. They are in their twenties and they drink with wild abandon. Eva, the drunkest of the trio, should have been sent home long ago.

"We've been hanging out with those Irish guys over at that table. We met them in Ibiza a few days ago," Abbey explains.

"Some of them are nice. Some of them just abandoned their wives and kids to come here to get drunk and party," Claire hisses.

I nod. "Then you're going to hate us. We came for the same reasons."

They laugh.

"We love our girlfriends and all," I explain, "but these are my childhood best friends. When I'm with them, I feel this energy and bond that makes me feel alive."

"Ha!" Claire scoffs with a theatrical eye roll. She doesn't believe a word I say.

"I'm not bullshitting you. It's the truth."

Justin, DJ, Brian, Lulu, and I didn't know each other from birth. We were born in the same year and ended up at the same school. Among eighty other kids, any of whom could have become our best friends. The five of us grew close not by coincidence, but by the choices we made. When Justin and I first decided to travel the summer of our twentieth birthday, we extended the invitation to others, but only Brian, DJ (still Pierre back then), and Lulu came through. Those four weeks on the road wove a single yarn of friendship, upon which new strands have been added over time. Every night out, every birthday party, every trip, strengthens the bond. Adult relationships work like gravitational pull—the closer you are, the stronger the pull, and the closer you grow.

I walk up to the Giroud-lookalike. I get right to the point.

"Hey man, my friends think you look like Giroud."

"Giroud?" he smiles. "Who's that?"

He pulls out his phone to fire up Google, but he blows his cover by spelling "Olivier Giroud" correctly.

Nice try, my friend. My good-looking friend.

But at least he's humble about it.

We have taken over the party. Sensing the tide is finally changing in our favor, DJ signals for more alcohol.

"DJ, what are you doing?" I ask.

"A party needs vodka just like our body needs blood."

Giroud delivers his Crystal Head Vodka. Our guests take turns posing for pictures with the crystal skull bottle.

"We are not splitting it, DJ," Brian insists.

Whenever we go clubbing and get bottle service, we split the bill evenly among the guys. Girls and girlfriends don't pay. We have done it this way for years. We feel it's a gentlemanly thing to do. But DJ has always found that sexist.

"It's like billionaires hiring models on their yachts," he once said.

One year for his birthday, he booked out a rooftop bar. In his Facebook invite, he told everyone that it was HK$500 per person, guys and girls alike. Only a handful of girls showed up. Back then, we all thought DJ was just being a CB. With years of hindsight and the current context of the world, I start to see his viewpoint now. Even in high-tech, one of the most male-centric fields, many of my colleagues and bosses are female. If I invite them out and offer to pay for them, I fear they would be offended. Is it a cultural difference between Hong Kong and America? Or is it the changing of times? I look over at DJ, who is now lying down on someone else's daybed, sandwiched between a Spanish couple, totally in his element. Who is he? Thought leader or CB?

The crowd starts trickling out at sunset, but we stay long after the music ends. As the pool party comes to a close, another rager begins in a nearby bar.

"Drink up boys!" Dave shouts, handing out shots of tequila to our friends from Valencia. The energy of this island. The power of youth!

Dave and DJ stay behind—last men standing again—while the rest leave for food. Among the plethora of food options along the boardwalk, we pick Thai. Over some overpriced pad see ew, we discuss after-dinner plans. We were tipped that Wayne Rooney would be at Eden tonight.

"Can we trust Vincent?" Kenny asks, his hair dripping with sweat after six hours of day-drinking.

Brian is quiet, a telltale sign he's ready for bed.

"Ken-Jai," Justin says, locking gaze with Kenny, "it's Wayne Rooney, man."

In a different time, on a different night, we would have gone in a heartbeat. What do we have to lose? In our twenties, we would order a round of *Long-lun* and get right back at it.

But that was a different time. In our battered state now,

sleep seems the most appealing. If no one will man up and suggest the obvious, I will do the devil's work.

"Even if he's there," I go out on a limb, "he is probably with his wife. We won't be able to get close. Let's go home and go hard tomorrow night."

They brutalize me for my lack of adventure, and then happily hop in a taxi home.

.

15

BAD NEPHEW — IBIZA

I AM A MARVELOUS HOUSEKEEPER. EVERY TIME I LEAVE A MAN I
KEEP HIS HOUSE. –ZSA ZSA GABOR

I WAKE up in a cold sweat.

Twelve hours till my aunt arrives. I need to get through this one night before handing the place over to my family.

This house is in no state for my sweet Goo-ma. Never underestimate the damage seven men can do to a house.

I jolt out of bed and scramble to the living room. The place looks like it rained junk food overnight.

Cloudy with a chance of honey BBQ chips.

A pair of jeans is balled up on the kitchen floor. A fallen Solo cup pyramid is scattered on our dining table. Beer and water puddles everywhere on the hardwood floor. Other than that, the house is in total peace. Everyone is still sleeping.

I begin my one-man mission.

I throw all my sheets and towels in the wash and try to pick out the laundry detergent from an entire shelf of cleaning agents. They all have instructions in different languages—French, Spanish, Italian, Arabic—probably left behind by past occupants.

Next—the floor. I fill up the mop bucket, and try my luck with that shelf again. I start with the first-floor bathroom and work my way around this two-thousand-square-foot house. All the while, my mom is bombarding me with WhatsApp messages.

Any good restaurant recommendation for Ibiza? What should we do?

I don't know, man. We just partied. Do your own research.

My brother Clement also texts me. He is arriving tonight, and he can't wait to party.

I take one swift look at the kitchen. Empty beer bottles occupy every inch of counter space. Sho's instant chicken cordon bleu has hardened on tin foil. The sink, which was cleared just yesterday, is stacked full of soiled dishes again. Let's save the kitchen for last.

The washing machine rumbles to a stop and rings its little finishing tune. It's hardly been thirty minutes; I must have selected the wrong cycle. I extract the load anyway and hang them to dry outside. The sun is already sizzling at 9 a.m. Under the morning ray the white sheets now shimmer with a hint of blue. Perhaps I should have separated the whites from the bright turquoise blue towels.

Things are off to a great start.

When Clement gets here tonight, he better help me clean up this mess.

"Oh, you guys are up already," I say, spotting DJ and Brian on the living room couch.

"Mmmhmm," they mumble without lifting their eyes from their phones.

I begin to vacuum the floor.

"Are you guys going to our primary school gathering in July?" DJ shouts over the noise of vacuum cleaner.

"Nope," Brian shouts back.

"I would if I were in Hong Kong," I say. "Haven't seen people from primary school for over a decade. I'm jealous you guys get to go."

"Meh," Brian replies.

"You better be super nice if you go. Don't just form your own small circle and act all cool," I say.

We spent our formative years at a Christian school in Hong Kong where we learned to live by modesty and integrity. Our past three days weren't quite befitting of those values. Ibiza bar crawl, Neon Paint party, fighting outside a Subway, pool party bottle service, jumbo sushi platter ... our old teachers would be disappointed.

We venture to the northern tip of the island for lunch. When we start to head back, Kenny is nowhere to be found.

"DJ, where did Kenny go?" I ask, waiting in the taxi, meter running.

"He said he's getting alcohol. Oh here he comes."

Kenny runs toward us with stuff falling out of his pockets left and right. In one hand he is carrying plastic bags of beer, in the other a bottle of sparkling wine.

"They've a supermarket here?" I ask.

"No. The restaurant sells them to-go," he replies, still catching his breath.

"Who's drinking that?" Brian asks, pointing to the cheap sparkly stuff.

"I just want to saber a champagne bottle with a machete," Kenny explains.

We look at him wide-eyed.

"Have you done this before?" Justin asks. "Where're you getting a machete?"

"Don't we have one at the villa?" Kenny replies.

Some people's brains are wired differently.

Another night in Ibiza, another packet of yellow powder drink. Another group doping session in the kitchen.

"Remember when Captain Tsubasa played through an injured shoulder on painkillers in the championship match? That's how I feel right now," I wince, referencing our favorite soccer comic books.

Everyone nods and chokes back various concoctions of herbal medicines. We have literally partied ourselves to the edge of pain.

"I'm hurting everywhere," Justin whimpers, removing a glass of warm water from the microwave.

It's our last night in Ibiza. DJ Hardwell is headlining at Ushuaïa. I approach this party with a sense of destiny. Tonight isn't about personal pleasure; it's about being out there for the boys. No matter the challenge, we forge on. Ushuaïa, here we come.

When we arrive at Ushuaïa, the opening act is playing to a ghost crowd. The 6 p.m. sun still feels like an inferno, and there is no shade at our table.

"Oh, Hardwell doesn't come on until ten," Justin says, reading the schedule.

"Let's come back later. Our place is only five minutes away," Sho suggests.

He has a point. Why languish under the sun before the main act? As they say in soccer, champions peak at the right time.

We return around 9:30 to a packed house. The place is buzzing. Justin waves the server over and orders a deadly amount of alcohol.

"Paying for a VIP table and partying only for two hours ... So *Fu-yee-doy*. Don't let my dad know," Justin sighs as he signs the credit card slip.

We gawk at the armory of alcohol that no one wants to drink. Kenny pours a round of vodka shots.

"Alright lads," Kenny yells. "Let's go."

Feeling a little homesick, Sho meets two girls from Macau and introduces them to the group.

"What are you girls doing here?" I ask.

"We're about to graduate college in the UK," Janice says, not exactly answering my question.

I gulp at the idea that they're almost a decade younger than us. Janice's friend Emily is already playing drinking games with DJ. Perhaps they both need their fixing of Chinese food.

Outside the bathroom, I strike up an unlikely friendship with Cristian, a Spanish MMA fighter training for his shot at the big time on Saturday, September 10, in England. He's about my size, but far denser. We exchange contacts. I ask him to remember me when he gets into the UFC.

"You should stop partying and drinking if you want to make it," I tell him, sounding like his mom.

He shrugs and gives me a bro hug.

When I return to our table, we have polished off every bottle. Dave, Sho, and Kenny are nowhere to be found.

"DJ, why are your arms all red?"

"I was playing a drinking game with Emily but she doesn't want to drink. So she proposed physical punishment instead."

I look over at Emily. Her arms are lobster red from DJ's slapping. Try explaining that to the police.

Hardwell finishes to a standing ovation from an energized audience. From the safety of our VIP table, I watch the sweaty crowd scream and dance like the world ends tonight. It is a magnificent sight. I've never understood the money DJs make. But tonight, standing among thousands enchanted by Hardwell's magic touch, I get it.

With my ears still ringing, I leave the club to find my brother, Clement, who has just landed in Ibiza with my aunt and cousin.

"Where're we going?" Clement asks, fixing his hair in front of a window. He's ready to party.

Everyone is off doing their own thing. Justin and Brian are eating sushi. DJ and Emily go for a swim in the ocean. Sho and Dave continue the party at Zanzibar with their new Korean friends. Kenny slots himself among a group of tough-looking guys at the next table over.

"Yo," Kenny mumbles into my ear when I turn up with Clement. With a huge smile on his face, he says, "I'm taking shots with the Italian mafia."

He invites me to sit down, but I don't want to waste energy making small talk. So Clement and I order two pints from the bar.

"Where's Virginia?" I ask. "Isn't she coming out?"

Virginia is our cousin from New Jersey, a precocious child with a steadfast passion for science and medicine. She knew how airplanes worked as a six-year-old. When her friends were dressing up their Barbies, she was building Gundams. School came easily for her; science competitions were her stomping ground. Outside of school, she did Chinese painting, Chinese calligraphy, and Chinese school. Her only indulgence was video games, which she played responsibly. I think I'm the only bad influence in her life.

She's my aunt's only child. When she left for Tufts after eighteen years under her mother's careful tutelage, Virginia added a rough edge to her personality. She drank every day, or so she told Clement and me. I don't believe it, nor do I believe she would ever do anything irresponsible. Maybe she was just trying to better connect with her cousins.

Still, Clement and I put her to the test when she visited Hong Kong one Christmas. We went out clubbing one night. Without saying goodbye, she left the club to get food with DJ and our friend Tiff. She got home before 3 a.m. I stayed out till 8 a.m. and spent Christmas Day in pain.

Gerald: 1. Virginia: 0.

She's like a sister to Clement and me—a sister who can't hang until 8 a.m.—but a sister nonetheless.

"She says she didn't feel like partying," Clement says.

"C'mon man. We're in Ibiza," I say with a theatrical eye roll. It won't dawn on me till much later that maybe she wanted to keep her mother company.

"She's at home with Goo-ma now," Clement says.

The thought of my aunt sobers me up like sticking my hand in an ice bucket.

"Did Goo-ma say anything?" I ask the dreaded question.

"When we arrived, Goo-ma asked 'why doesn't Gerald open the door for us?'"

My *Goo-ma* is traditional when it comes to etiquette—reciprocate people's kindness; respect your elders; send a gift even if you can't attend the wedding. Because Clement, our cousin Wendy, and I all attended high school and college on the East Coast, she became our caretaker through those years. She paid our bills and took care of our finances. She attended our parent-teacher conferences and my piano recitals. She knew our housemasters by name. She read all our report cards. Every summer she drove us back from school and let us cram her attic with all our stuff. With her flying all the way to Ibiza from the US, an airport pickup would have been the right thing to do. Instead, I hid the villa key in a bush and left a note. We didn't have any food left in the house either—at least that she would eat. Some nephew I am.

"I opened the champagne in the fridge for her. There's only beer and tap water in the house," Clement says, reminding me of Kenny's machete project that he never got around to.

I dread the explaining I'll have to do in the morning. But there's nothing I can do now. I pound my beer and try to enjoy the rest of the night.

"Where to, guys?" I ask when the crew reunite.

"That one," Dave points to the massive club across the street called Space.

"Let's go," DJ says, taking charge.

I give Goo-ma and Virginia my bedroom and sleep in the

second living room instead. The next morning, I stay in bed for as long as possible to delay the inevitable. My pathetic attempt to clean came undone when eight drunk men returned from Space last night and pillaged the place. The living room is covered in sand from DJ's shoes. All the food is still left out on the kitchen counter. Our flight leaves in the early afternoon. Before that, I need to make sure the cleaners show up to give this place a makeover. I will also need to pick up my mother from the airport just to brief her on what she's about to see. Inviting my family to the villa seemed like a good idea at the time. But now that I'm sleep-deprived, hungover, and sick, it's the last thing I want to deal with. With these thoughts weighing on my mind, I get out of bed and greet my aunt at the pool.

"Hello, Goo-ma!" I cheer with all the enthusiasm I can muster.

"Hi, Gerald," my aunt replies.

I can never tell if she's disapproving or not, especially after I've done something bad. I'm having that same uneasy feeling now as I did every Thanksgiving at her place when I was still in my pajamas five minutes before dinner and had done nothing all day but video games.

Virginia waves me a cool hello. I lean away as we hug in hopes that they won't still smell the alcohol. We were close when I studied on the East Coast, but they don't know this side of me—at least not to this degree.

"How do you like this place?" I ask, slathering sunblock on my shoulders and giving myself an excuse not to look her in the eye. Whatever the situation, sun protection comes first.

"Oh it's a beautiful place," my aunt says.

I smile. "Glad you like it. You should have seen it before I cleaned it yesterday. I cleaned the first-floor bathroom just for you guys."

The place is a disaster; I am not fooling anyone. But I want them to know that I tried.

"Actually I think we'll move to the upstairs bathroom when you guys leave. The first floor one is all moldy."

I thought it smelled a little mildewy after I mopped the floor, and was hoping the smell would go away once everything dried.

"Oh I'm sorry. I think I used the wrong stuff to clean," I say.

Virginia shakes her head. "No. It's moldy from the inside. You can smell it. No reason risking some nasty respiratory stuff from the mold," Virginia adds.

In the delirium of hangover, I don't know how to respond. Who am I to question a future doctor?

"How's med school, Virginia?" I ask, changing topic.

Some people become doctors for the money and prestige. Virginia, I believe, truly wants to make a difference in the world.

"It's the hardest thing you've ever done times ten," she says.

I nod. If DJ were to say something like that, we would argue forever. But with family and especially in front of my aunt, I keep my mouth shut. Respect your elders, and their kids, if the elders are around.

"We haven't eaten since yesterday," Goo-ma says.

Oh shit.

We have run out of food. I am banking on Clement to figure out the food situation when he gets up.

"We still have some chicken cordon bleu left over from last night," I joke.

She doesn't find it funny. DJ chooses this moment to come out to my rescue.

"Oh, hi, Pierre," my aunt smiles and gives him a hug.

"You remember him?" I ask, shocked.

"Of course, he stayed with us in 2008. Right before you guys flew to Europe."

DJ has a way of making an impression on people. My aunt has the memory of an elephant. The last time my family and hers went on a vacation was to France in 1996. We talk about it fondly every time I see her.

I'm sure this Ibiza trip will be talked about for years, albeit for entirely different reasons.

I barge into every room to strip the sheets and throw them in the wash. I have arranged for cleaners to come before my mother arrives this afternoon, but they aren't answering my messages. The fear of being stood up propels me to start vacuuming in a panic.

"Gerald," Goo-ma looks at me, sniffing my apprehension. "Are the cleaners coming?"

Her tone was serious and firm.

"Oh...yes of course," I stutter in feigned confidence as I continue to vacuum maniacally like a rogue housekeeping robot. "Just tidying up a bit. Haha."

My friends aren't sharing my urgency or offering any help. Justin makes scrambled eggs, but is otherwise useless at housework. And Dave doesn't even cook.

"So who's carrying the belt?" Dave asks no one in particular. Everyone wants to win the belt, but no one actually wants to carry it around. Because he won the belt from me, technically I should carry it. But I don't feel like doing anything for him.

Ask me, Dave. I dare you.

We are slowly wearing on each other. Even petty things like deciding who carries the communal shampoo is becoming a source of tension. Not sleeping doesn't help, and we are all homesick. I start to tune out and stop caring about things, like whether the cleaners will show up, or whether I should separate colors and whites in the wash. I don't even bother to lock my suitcase anymore. The built-in TSA lock on my suitcase has been broken since Amsterdam. I sit through a five-minute YouTube video on how to repair it but decide that there is nothing worth stealing anyway.

I walk to the airport with Clement to pick up my mother and Peter. I fall asleep in the arrival hall until my mom wakes me up.

"You look terrible," she comments.

"Nice to see you, too."

Clement picks up his rental car and drives us back to the villa. I give them a quick tour of the place.

"Wow, this looks great. Thank you for letting us stay," my mom says, choosing to focus on the positives. She's tiptoeing around the mess we've left behind, both figuratively and literally.

"So what time are you guys leaving?" she asks, poking a stale chicken cordon bleu left on the counter with a stick like it's a dead squirrel.

"Any moment now. Our flight leaves in two hours," I say, zipping up my backpack. I'm so exhausted that I have even lost my paranoia with time.

She seems offended that I didn't plan to spend more time with her.

"Trust me. You don't want us around."

She doesn't answer. We stare at Sho and Dave trying to squeeze in one last round of beer pong.

"Where are you guys off to next?" she asks.

"Pamplona. Then Madrid. Then home," I say.

"Pamplona!?" she yells, her eyes bulging. "You never told me! You're not doing the bull run, are you?"

I shrug. "I don't know."

"*Lok Lok*," she calls me by my Chinese name, "please don't do something dangerous. I'll be very worried."

The bull run was Kenny's idea; I was going to play it by ear. But now that she has asked me not to do it, I *have* to do it, right?

"We've gone too far to stop now," I say, my cryptic reply seeming more befitting of a serial killer.

I hug my family goodbye and head to the airport.

The cleaners finally text me back and say they will be there in the afternoon.

Brian and Kenny change into their soccer jerseys at the airport. DJ is now donning a suit in thirty-plus-degree heat.

"You guys really doing it?" I ask.

They nod, giggling.

"I want no part in this," I say.

"Yo, it's a shuttle! It's a shuttle!" Kenny chirps when he notices that we won't be boarding via jetway. It is usually an inconvenience, but not today.

We hang back on the shuttle so we'll be the last to board.

When the stage is set, Kenny, Brian, and DJ sprint to the top of the plane airstair. On my signal, they begin their slow descent. With Bose headphones wrapped around his neck, DJ waves to an imaginary crowd. The idea is to mimic soccer stars exiting their team jet on international duty, usually in Armani suits and carrying a man purse. DJ doesn't have a man purse, so he is using Justin's black toiletry bag. I wish I had captured the look of utter bewilderment of the airline staff.

"Hurry up guys!" I yell, urging them to wrap things up before we get in trouble.

"Oh my god, we did it!" Kenny cackles as he bounces his way up the airstair again, this time to board the plane.

"Hey send me the pictures," DJ demands.

I haven't even settled into my seat yet. He uploads them on Facebook before takeoff.

I sleep the entire flight to Barcelona and wake up more tired. If my body were an iPhone, I am at about 10 percent.

As the rest of us continue our journey, it is time for Sho to say goodbye.

"You sure you want to leave now?" I ask.

"No, but I need to visit my godfather in Cardiff. And before that I want to spend a few days in Barcelona."

"We'll miss you," I say, doing our secret handshake.

"Move back to Hong Kong man," he replies.

Waiting in line to recheck our bags, we see five Hong Kong teenagers up ahead.

"They are just like us ten years ago," Justin says.

The one with orange highlights and calling the shots is Justin. The dorky one with white-rimmed glasses is Lulu. The one with the crazy hair is DJ. The one holding a whole plastic bag of snacks is obviously Brian. I'm the guy who is taking care of business at the counter.

"We were way cooler than them," Brian says.

"They look like little punks," I say. Maybe we came across that way too back then.

We head to our most perilous destination—Pamplona.

♦

SHO'S FROZEN CHICKEN CORDON BLEU RECIPE

1. Preheat oven to 375°F (or 191°C)
2. Remove frozen entrée from pouch
3. Line baking tray with aluminum baking sheet
4. Place entrée on baking sheet at least 3 inches apart
5. Bake 1-2 entrées for 38-40 minutes. Bake 3-6 entrées for 40-42 minutes (or the duration of two games of FIFA)
6. Serve them on the tray straight from the oven

16

ARKHAM CITY — IBIZA, PAMPLONA

ALL CRUELTY SPRINGS FROM WEAKNESS. –LUCIUS ANNAEUS
SENECA

OUR PLANE LANDS in Pamplona Airport against the most picturesque backdrop of open meadows and distant hills. Golden fields shimmer in the late afternoon sun. We are instructed to get off the plane and walk straight into the terminal, but everyone is idling on the tarmac, startled by this place's beauty. Perhaps this is why they put up a "no picture" sign on the tarmac.

"All the taxi drivers are wearing white and red," Brian points out.

When we arrive downtown, we realize it's not just the taxi drivers—everyone in town is in San Fermín attire. Every single person except us.

Today is the first day of San Fermín. We drag our roller luggage through two hundred meters of party mayhem to find our Airbnb host among a vast red-and-white sea. Sally greets Kenny with a sloppy hug, making no attempt to disguise the fact that she has been drinking all day.

"Oh this is Marco," she purrs, stroking her male companion's arm. The smirk on Marco's face tells me he is neither her husband nor boyfriend.

Kenny begins his small talk.

"So Sally, you're Canadian right? How did you end up in Pamplona?"

Years ago when her study abroad was drawing to a close, Sally wasn't ready to go back to Canada. She exhausted every avenue to stay, and made one last plea to her parents for a brief stop in Spain.

"I told them I wanted to learn Spanish," she slurs.

She fell in love with the country and settled down in Pamplona. The rest is history.

She is exceedingly friendly in a drunk person way. She laughs at your jokes and seems interested in everything you have to say.

Her three-bedroom apartment has plenty of space to accommodate all of us. To charge three thousand euros for two nights is a lesson in supply and demand. Such is the draw of San Fermín.

I consult the Internet for the origin of San Fermín. It appears to involve a third-century Pamplona native named Fermín, whose legacy goes something like this: Born to a family of power in Pamplona during the Roman times, Fermín converted to Christianity under the stewardship of French Bishop San Saturnino. Fueled by his ardent devotion to the religion, Fermín set off for France to further his training. He would return to Pamplona as its first bishop. His subsequent treks proved less fortunate. He hung out with the wrong crowd in France, which led to his beheading in Amiens. He died a martyr; San Fermín is a celebration in his memory.

Later on, it was decided that San Fermín would become a massive weeklong party featuring bullfighting and bull running, some say in remembrance of the fact that San Fermín was dragged to death on the streets with bulls running after him. That seems too convenient to be true. Besides, wasn't he beheaded? There are a thousand questions in my head. Anyhow, the festival was permanently moved from October to July in 1591 for better weather, giving further credence to this not being about Fermín at all. Sorry, San Fermín, the world is for the living.

"Hey, can you tell us about the bull run?" Kenny asks.

Sally puts down her drink and takes a poignant breath. "Okay, let me tell you from a mom's perspective."

She takes another deep breath and puts her hand on Kenny's shoulder.

"These bulls are veeerrry big and veeeeerrry fierce. More people should die," she warns, dragging out her qualifiers for emphasis.

She wants Kenny to heed her advice and reconsider. And when Kenny just stands there, urging her to continue, I sense a twinge of irritation from her. Kenny might be an easy, fun-loving guy, but when his mind is set on an idea, no one can talk him out of it.

"But if you want to do it," she continues, "I can give you the name of a bar. Runners like to go there to talk strategy."

That wasn't what we wanted to hear from a local. We wanted to hear that it is super fun and safe. But we are three thousand euros too deep to back out now. Besides, Kenny is going with or without us. He has a deep bucket list and intends to check off every item.

Sally also manages several properties along the bull run

route. They offer excellent viewing of the proceedings, she claims, should we decide to spectate instead. But at almost two hundred euros per person, Kenny says he'll "get back to her."

"Don't sit on it for too long because lots of people are asking about them," Sally smirks.

Something tells me *no one* is asking for those tickets.

When Kenny runs out of topics with Sally, she returns to the festivities. DJ grabs her on the way out for the Wi-Fi password.

"Yo, let's go check out the bull run route," Kenny suggests.

"Yes, and we need to get the festival gear," Dave echoes.

I don't want to be anywhere near the crowd.

"Come on, let's go. Don't stay here by yourself," Brian urges.

I am glad I join them. We stop for kebabs around the corner from our place. The portion is generous, and after all day of traveling, a greasy meat dish is just what I need.

I've been in some dirty places in my life, often on my own volition. I have stayed at many rustic hostels around the world. In college, my fraternity house basement was flooded every weekend with beer. I'm a season ticket holder of the Oakland Raiders whose stadium bathroom at halftime is best described as a "free for all." I spend almost every New Year's Eve in Lan Kwai Fong, Hong Kong's nightlife central.

All this is to say I have seen some shit.

Pamplona during *San Fermín*, however, is next level. The entire city stinks of stale alcohol. People chase and squirt each other from their sangria "sac." We might have trashed our Ibiza villa, but our clothes are off-limits. The marble streets are sticky from dried sangria and have turned into one giant glue trap. Mountains of garbage pile up into makeshift bunkers. Anarchy is on full display when a fight breaks out in Plaza del Ayuntamiento. Two groups of red-blooded men are having a full go at each other before an indifferent crowd. Whole minutes pass without someone jumping in to break it up. There is no policeman in sight. The news channel cameraman just keeps filming. Firecrackers go off like gunshots at random intervals. This is Arkham City without Batman. Pure pandemonium.

And people do get hurt during the alcohol-fueled fiesta. Hundreds have taken to the streets in protest of assaults against women during San Fermín. I wonder if the festival outfit makes it hard to catch the assailants. Even as a group of grown men, we have to be cautious.

"Yo, let's go buy the San Fermín outfit now," Dave repeats with urgency.

Heads nod all around. Blending in with this drunk, belligerent crowd is now a matter of personal safety. The last thing we want is to be picked on for being different.

We storm into the closest store and emerge with white pants, T-shirts, and red bandanas.

"Much better," we exhale.

"Let's scout out the course," Kenny suggests.

The entire course runs a mere 875 meters; most bull runs conclude within three minutes. It ends at the coliseum where the bulls will be locked up until the afternoon bullfight. Many other daredevil runners are scouting out the course like us.

We nod to each other. "Good luck tomorrow."

At Plaza del Castillo, a live band plays to a young crowd

singing and partying with wild abandon. No one is spared from the sangria rain. At 11 p.m. the party is just getting started. We are about to head to bed; the previous week has done a number on us. I don't believe in stereotypes, but if the Asians are good at math and the Irish can drink, then the Spanish can party.

Every corner we turn, there is a party in full swing luring us to go in. This festival is crazier than we imagined, but not in a fun way. Tonight, it feels like arriving late to a party where everyone is already drunk. And if we go out tonight and blow whatever is left in our tank, I fear we won't make it till the end.

We head home at the stroke of midnight. We have a big day ahead.

We go to bed still undecided on the bull run. Kenny and DJ are in for sure. Brian and I will follow the group. Dave is noncommittal. Justin wouldn't mind a rain out.

We wake up to the symphony of multiple alarm clocks and drizzle. It's 6 a.m.

Nobody slept. Anxiety and drunken chatter from the street kept us up all night. We gather in the living room to weigh our options. As if bull running alone isn't dangerous enough, there is the slick cobblestone street to worry about now in the rain. Some of us just want to go back to bed.

"Let's just go there and check it out," Kenny suggests.

We scramble to comb our hair into submission and make our way toward the town hall plaza.

"This is the widest part of the whole thing," Dave explains.

We picked this to be our starting point during our scouting mission last night.

There is already a crowd. Some are early risers like us; others have been up all night, evident from their body odor and speech clarity. It is still dark and shockingly chilly. DJ is wearing his dress shirt as a jacket, buttoned all the way. With the red scarf, he looks like our *stroopwafel* chef from Amsterdam. I could use a *stroopwafel* now.

"DJ, are these your camera glasses?" I ask.

He and Brian are wearing matching eyeglasses with thick black end pieces. They are the ugliest glasses I have ever seen.

"Yeah. Got them from Taobao. Eighty minutes of battery life and 160 minutes of recording," he says.

The bull run doesn't start until eight, but by 6:20 a.m., a small crowd has formed outside the town hall. The wooden fences that outline the course have been erected overnight, though the gate is still open to let people come and go as they please. Once the runners have reached a certain number, that, too, will be closed off. What we come to realize is that once inside the fence, you are blocked in. There is no such thing as checking it out; we're in.

"Mmm ... I guess we're doing this," Justin says, still trying to process what just happened.

Choices are usually good, but in some situations, I prefer the decision to be made for me and I just have to focus on how to cope.

With more than an hour and a half to go, we stand there and talk strategy. In these close quarters, we come to know the mix of personalities around us. First, people who preface everything by listing their chronic injuries—broken hands, cracked ribs, sprained ankles. Excuse makers exist in all walks of life.

Then, there are fearless drunks who show up wearing sandals.

"Stay away from those disaster magnets," I scoff.

Lastly, there are the likable cowards like Australian Greg.

"I'm happy just to make it out unscathed," he admits.

We nod.

"Let's just hide here and play it safe," we say, pointing at our communal sissy corner. Smart people live. Brave ones don't always. That's just how the world works.

Last but not least, there are Americans who compare everything to America.

"This place is Times Square New Year's Eve times ten," one American in his fifties says. He is a repeat participant of San Fermín.

By his side is a rookie whose middle name has to be "Regret."

"I had a chance to do it in 1974 but went to Marseille instead. I've been regretting it ever since," he sighs. Today he is fulfilling a dream forty-two years in the making.

Brian is standing hunched forward, looking all fidgety. The constant readjustment of his position doesn't seem to offer any relief.

"You alright man? You look constipated."

"Yeeaah," he stammers, "I need to take a shit."

A sadness washes over me, something I rarely feel with this group of people. "Dude, I feel so bad for you. I can't image a worse time."

He nods a pained, helpless nod. I can see him clenching his fists in his pockets.

I find the diversity of personalities interesting. It's all part of the experience. I could do without the secondhand smoke, though.

The clock is ticking at snail pace. Perhaps the most excruciating part is the wait. With less than an hour to go, the policemen shut the gate to the course.

"*Mañana*," they yell to the latecomers. Better wake up earlier tomorrow.

During the torturous final thirty minutes, firecrackers, which we mistake to be the starting signal of *encierro*, go off at random intervals and send us into panic. Policemen begin to boot out the physically unfit or apparent liabilities. Those donning any kind of wearable cameras are also asked to leave. Are they worried about people getting hurt trying to take videos? Or something unsightly being caught on tape? DJ's eyeglasses camera escapes their scrutiny, as does this young Spaniard with a GoPro duct-taped to his chest underneath his T-shirt.

Meanwhile, spectators watch from the balcony above, enjoying breakfast from a safe distance and hoping for bloodshed. This is almost like *the Hunger Games*; we're all Mockingjays. Brian is a Mockingjay ready to shit his pants.

With fifteen minutes to go, the police open up the partitions to create more running room.

"Move! Move!" a policeman yells.

We cling to our sissy corner for dear life as a troop of elite-looking runners pass through. They march along showing no signs of nerves. The ones in the front look like they have nothing to lose. Following behind are the "pros," donning jerseys and hardened looks in their eyes. They look ready for war. We wait in relentless vigilance.

At 8 a.m. sharp, with a lack of ceremony that feels almost anticlimactic, the first rocket goes off.

The bulls are released.

A panic washes over the crowd.

We can't see more than a couple of feet in front of us; the crowd's reaction is our only window to the world. I never knew that the collective gasp of hundreds in close quarters could be this terrifying.

We are *petrified*.

A second rocket goes off, signaling the release of the last bull from the corral. The hysteria escalates to a different level. The plaza crowd begins to scamper as runners from the starting line reach us in a frantic sprint. Their body language can be described in two words—horror and desperation.

"I'm out! I'm out!" a girl in yoga pants pleads and hops over the fence to safety.

Our eyes can't see, but we feel the rumbling of the ground. The bulls' steps are penetrating, urgent, and markedly uniform. We are frozen in place as if confronted by an advancing army. I hear bodies tumbling on the cobblestone street. I hear that muffled gasp people make when they are beyond frightened.

"Run! Run! Run!" the policeman yells.

And then we take off.

Runners who started in the middle of the course scamper for dear life to the sides. Those of us on the flank are squished and trampled on.

I take off.

I turn to look for my friends when a heavy mass zooms by. I count six. Six light-beige-colored bulls so big they block the sun. Their heavy bells jingle in perfect synchrony with their powerful strides. They are marching down the middle with laser focus, a far cry from the man-hunting I have seen on YouTube. I allow myself to imagine being rolled under this moving blob of destruction and coming out as my favorite dish—steak tartare. What would the world be without me?

"Let's go!!!" DJ screams from the pack in his unmistakable serial killer camera glasses.

I reach for him but the crowd knocks us apart.

"Take the inner turn!" DJ yells out as I approach the infamous ninety-degree turn. Research footage has shown that most people get gored at that outer corner. I watch as a drunken, sandal-wearing idiot slips and wipes out.

Study up, my friend.

The arena is a mere three hundred meters ahead, but danger lurks with every step. All of a sudden, another wave of terror propagates from behind us. DJ and I exchange a nervous look—it must be the second set of bulls.

"Waaaaa!!!!" We dodge to the side as a powerful force pushes past us. DJ's glasses fly off and shatter on the ground.

We survived two close calls. All the bulls have passed. Now that we are home free, we gun for the arena to beat the closing gate. Those who make it in gets to play tag with the bulls for a bit.

But do I really want that? I ask myself.

We don't make it.

We watch the gates close from a distance following the passing of the last bull. A third rocket goes off, signaling the end of the run. The whole thing lasts just over three minutes.

"You guys okay?" DJ asks as the rest of the group crosses the finish line.

They nod, still in shock. They look unscathed.

I look to the spectators above; their obvious disappointment delights me. They paid hundreds of euros expecting to see a goring or two.

All told, only four hospitalizations and no goring on day one of 2016 San Fermín.

A peaceful day by its bloody standard.

"Let's take some pictures by the 'Running of the Bulls' statue," DJ says.

"Okay, okay. Hurry up," Brian groans.

When we get back to the apartment, Brian sprints to the bathroom. Everyone else crawls back into bed.

"Yo, Sally is telling us to check out the Giants and Big Heads parade from our balcony." Kenny jostles us awake later in the morning.

He pulls back the curtain and lets too much light in. We hear drums and trumpets.

This is like the Macy's Thanksgiving Day parade with less fanfare. Led by the marching band, eight pairs of giant figures represent the kings and queens of Europe, Asia, America, and Africa. They dance along with seventeen smaller characters in big-head masks wielding foam truncheons.

"Ha, why are they whacking the children?" I ask. I wave to the people on the balcony across from us.

Kenny shrugs.

We go back to bed.

Under the pretense of checking in on us, Sally stops by the apartment in the afternoon to visit her latest love interest, Kenny. We let Kenny handle all affairs Sally. Some of us want to do the bull run again, and we want to ask if she can take photos of us. Perhaps a little charm offensive on Sally will do the trick?

"Hey Sally," Prince Charming Kenny says. "You won't happen to be watching the run from your balcony tomorrow, will you?"

Her eyes glow. A cheeky smile crosses on her face.

"Look guys, let me give you the deal of your life," she mutters in a low voice, ready to divulge the secret of the universe. "Just eighty-five euros per person for the balcony. You won't find a better deal."

She thought that we wanted to buy her balcony tickets! Enough with those already!

"Forget it Kenny," I mumble in Cantonese. She is one relentless saleswoman.

"Oh wow, thanks Sally!" Kenny squeaks in feigned surprise. "Let me get back to you in an hour?"

The political savvy of this boy. He is going places.

We spend our first leisurely afternoon since Ibiza. We just lounge about and drift in and out of sleep. We drink pitchers of sangria and eat potato and egg tapas for a late lunch at Plaza del Castillo. Let it be known that Justin's FaceTime obligation once again delays our group plans.

Shops all over town are selling professional grade photos from this morning's bull run. The shot of the day features a middle-aged Asian male sent airborne by a charging bull, his face twisted by the horn. If the man was after the total San Fermín experience, he has gotten his money's worth.

"Yo, yo, I found me!" Kenny shrieks.

It is a photo taken from the town hall plaza. From this

vantage point, there are even more people than we suspected. You really have to squint, but buried deep in that sissy corner is Waldo himself.

Kenny buys a few copies. Most customers just take pictures of the pictures on their smartphones. There are CBs everywhere in the world.

Rested and fed, we head out for the second event of today— bull fight. We paid several times the face value for these tickets. Sally explains that all bullfighting tickets are owned by families for generations, and they can charge as much as they want. It is still scorching at 6 p.m. and our warm sangria does little to cool us off. It is a magnificent scene in the arena. The entire place is packed with spectators in all white, waving red fans. This looks like movie choreography.

Almost everything I know about bullfighting comes from Hemingway's *The Sun Also Rises*. I'd read it years ago, and the only things I recall from the novel are the excessive drinking and partying, the love triangle between the protagonists, and the glorification of the young matador. I have always thought of bullfighting as a solo endeavor, but today I learn that it's anything but. The fight begins with three *banderilleros* performing a series of passes with the bull using their magenta-and-gold capes. This allows the matador to assess his target's aggression and quickness. Then, two *picadors* enter the fray on horses and pierce the bull's shoulder with their lances. This weakens the bull's back muscle and really pisses him off. The remarkable composure of these horses surprises me. Even with the blinders and heavy armor, I have to wonder, what is in it for the horses? Next, the *banderilleros* will return to plant two barbed sticks—*banderillas*—onto the bull's back to further handicap the animal.

By then, the bull is half dead.

Now the matador comes in for the finish.

If the buildup has been a team effort, the final act is a celebration of individuality. The matador's *traje de luces* is adorned with luxurious gold embroidery and it shimmers like shining armor. He stands in the center and takes a slow turn to see the whole arena, letting the bull and the whole world know that he is the only alpha in the ring. His every move is an ostentatious presentation of the sport. He starts off with passes with the bull while trying to look as effortless as possible. This matador likes to turn his back to the bull. The audience loves his taunt and showers him with applause at every flashy flick of his hair. The bull is already gushing blood no thanks to him, so what he's bragging about? After more of this cat-and-mouse game, the matador is handed his *estoques*—steel sword —for the finish. The idea is to maneuver the bull into position and stab it right through the shoulder blade into its heart, which is about the only humane thing in bullfighting. The arena holds its collective breath as the matador sets up for his finishing touch.

The bull charges on its final breath.

The matador swerves and drives his sword into the bull in one fluid motion.

But he misses.

The sword is wedged on the bull's back like an antenna, its heavy handle seesawing back and forth as the bull quivers in pain. The arena erupts in a cacophony of whistle.

"*Maricón!*" the Spaniard in front of us screams and kicks over a half-full sangria.

The matador looks unfazed and readies himself for the second try.

He lines up, dodges the charging bull, and plunges his *estoques* into the bull's back.

He succeeds this time around, burying three feet of steel into the bull's torso. I grimace as the bull coughs blood and tries to walk it off. After a few labored steps, he collapses to the ground. A *banderillero* rushes in to put a dagger through his brain. A group of men then ties the corpse onto a horse carriage and drags it on a victory lap. Some reward for fighting till the end. This sends the crowd into a frenzy, a stark contrast to our stunned reaction at the brutality.

"Damn," I murmur.

I look to my friends and no one knows what to make of what we just saw.

The second bullfight follows the same sequence—the *banderilleros*, the *picadors*, and the *matador*. The only difference is that this bull, who has the number 82 branded on his thigh, shows no desire to fight from the start. Maybe he saw the first bull on his way out. In bullfighting, this behavior poses a greater concern to the matador because it makes the bull unpredictable.

Escape, unfortunately, is not in the cards for 82. These bullfighters know just how to get a bull's attention. After the first blood is drawn, 82 is made fully aware that this is do-or-die for him. This matador, who looks more seasoned than the first, kicks off his shoes and takes showmanship to another level. He was conducting a TV interview right before entering the arena; perhaps the shoes are his coming good on what he has promised on camera. I find it hard to root for someone so arrogant, but he manages to back it up. His *estoques* finds the bull's heart on the first try, granting 82 a swift sendoff into the afterlife.

Tangled in this never-ending game of one-upmanship, the third matador, nineteen-year-old Peruvian Andrés Roca Rey, opts to fight on his knees. Unfortunately, this bull is too smart for his trickery. The bull sends Rey airborne and then delivers the bullfighting equivalent of ground and pound. The arena lets out a collective gasp as Rey braces himself in a fetal position against repeated goring. The other bullfighters and trainers rush in to his rescue. I later learn Rey enters the day with an unnerving record of goring—five times in the last five outings. Time for a new line of work, perhaps? But boy is he a fighter. He gets back on his feet, waves off his help, and fights on. He goes on to deliver the cleanest finish yet. So impressive is his recovery that the high-ranking official enters the arena and awards him the bull's ears for exemplary performance. Two ears and the tail are considered the highest honor, or *los máximo trofeos.*

There are three more fights left, but we've seen enough.

I can understand the appeal of bullfighting. But as much as I'm fascinated by the history, tradition, and showmanship, it just feels cruel and unfair. I think I've seen my last bullfight. This is probably my last San Fermín, and I'm okay with that.

We get takeout from our favorite kebab place and head home for France versus Germany.

The next day, Justin and I sit out the bull run while others return to Calle Santo Domingo for one final flourish.

"I'm going into the plaza today," DJ declares.

Freed from the prospect of death, I see a different side of

the bull run. First, all good viewing spots are gone after 6:30 a.m. Sally was right. For people who hate the crowd and can't wake up early, the balcony is the only spectating option. The older I get, the less I enjoy the touch of strangers, especially when sober and at 7:30 a.m. We hang back for more space, even if it means seeing only spectators' heads. They smell fresh from partying all night in the sewer. Ah, the joy of early twenties.

Five minutes before eight, two guys lean a crooked ladder against someone's window for a bird's-eyes view. This place really has no laws.

The first rocket goes off. Justin and I can't see anything, but we hear an unnerving "oooh" from the crowd. Two medics perched on the railings signal for help immediately.

"It's like in WWE when someone gets really hurt and the ref stops the match," Justin says, crisscrossing his forearms to imitate the WWE signal.

So what caused the commotion?

In TV replay later, we learn that a man was flipped by a bull in midair, landed on his head, and was gored.

Bull run trifecta achieved.

Described as one of the most dangerous runs in Pamplona history, day two of San Fermín 2016 concludes with sixteen hospitalizations. Seven people were gored. Our boys make it out fine. Only Dave needs minor medical attention.

"Injury?! You just scraped your knee!" Justin mocks.

"I'll be on the injury report tonight on the news. Representing Hong Kong," Dave says, holding up a victory sign. I guess that was his real objective.

They are lucky to walk away unharmed.

"These bulls were out for blood from the get-go," DJ explains.

"They just ran back and forth trying to hurt people," Brian adds.

To force forward progress, the policemen closed off sections of the course and turned the run into some kind of cage match between the bulls and runners. My friends all bailed out at various points.

"When I saw the bull running backwards toward us, that was it for me," Brian says.

After the bull run, a massive street cleaning army emerges to chase the drunks to bed, a daily handoff during San Fermín to restore Pamplona to temporary normalcy. We run into Sally with another guy. No wonder she never went back to Canada.

My mother texts me. *When you did the bull run, did you wear those white clothes everyone was wearing as I saw on the news?*

Yes, I reply.

Send me the video your friends shot, she writes.

Now that she knows we didn't get hurt, she wants to see the video.

Forty-eight hours is enough San Fermín for the lifetime. Our whirlwind tour of Pamplona comes to a close.

17

WISH HER HAPPINESS — MADRID

LIVING WELL IS THE BEST REVENGE. –GEORGE HERBERT

THE TRAIN STATION is crowded with Spanish teenagers in soiled San Fermín outfits, carrying their belongings in plastic bags. They look like they've partied for days without a shower or sleep. These Spanish kids can play.

We aren't looking any better ourselves. We still have one more night in Madrid, but we are limping toward the finish line.

Our train to Madrid is indefinitely delayed due to mechanical issues. On the platform, we sit on our luggage among hundreds of stranded passengers as the conductor attempts to resurrect his choo choo. Our ears perk up every time the train engine tries to come to life. And when the rumbling dies seconds later, we sigh.

I check in every so often with the station staff for an update, but all they can provide is a hand wave and an unapologetic smile. The train is "blocked," one woman always says. All announcements are in Spanish, and they refuse to commit to any timeline.

"Don't worry guys," Brian says. "If we get rescheduled on a

different train, we should have priority because we bought first class."

We smile, thankful that Brian has chosen not to be a CB this time.

"Worst case," I say, "we rent a car and drive to Madrid. We'd be there tonight."

We are in for a long wait. We may as well get some candy and get comfortable here. I binge on *ladrillos*. They are shaped like industrial electrical cables and taste like multiple sour laces bundled together. It makes my teeth hurt just thinking about them.

"Hey Justin, I'm planning a trip to Mongolia. Got any suggestions?" Kenny asks.

"Oh yeah," Justin says, reliving his windmill-counting trip back in his Big Four accounting days. "I went there and checked into those Mongolian yurts. They asked me if I wanted to upgrade to a private bathroom. I asked how much. They told me the equivalent of twenty Hong Kong dollars (less than three U.S. dollars). I said 'sure.' Then I went in to the 'private' bathroom and found eight turds already in the toilet."

We burst out laughing.

"You have to wonder," Justin says, "who would poop there when there are already six in the box?"

We talk about the horrific motel we stayed at in Kenya with the one-flush-wonder toilet and a shower that came down in a trickle. The romance of shoestring travel. After going days without meat, our guide put us up in a rundown motel with a small restaurant. We ordered every item on the menu. They were simple dishes, but they gave us *omakase* satisfaction. What we would do to relive that moment. Being stranded on this platform brings back that feeling.

A backup train arrives and we are finally off to Madrid. On the train they show the DreamWorks movie *Turbo*. I can hear the entire Adele album from Justin's headphone loud and clear across the aisle.

Get your ears checked, bro.

"So why didn't you run today?" DJ asks me.

"I don't know," I say. "I guess after the first day I just didn't feel like being part of the whole thing anymore."

"You know, I don't think I need to run in front of angry bulls to prove my courage."

"What do you mean?"

"I mean, it does take a lot of courage to do it. But if that's the whole point, why stop there? Why not outrun a tiger? Why not swim with sharks?" he says.

"Well, those are much harder to find in Spain, but I see your point."

"To be honest, I think I regret it a little bit now, especially knowing how much it costs to be part of the festival."

For DJ, everything always comes back to a financial equation.

"To me it feels like visiting North Korea," he continues. "It seems mysterious and exotic. But it is also funding a dictatorship spanning three generations and what this dictatorship has done to its people."

I just nod, too tired to partake in this intellectual debate.

"I also understand that it's a Spanish tradition, but I don't think tradition is an excuse for wrongdoing. There are many traditions we've abandoned—gladiator fighting, polygamy ..."

Bull fighting seems cruel and unnecessary to me too, but as a beef eater, do I get to judge?

· · ·

Our train arrives in Madrid at dusk. It's a gorgeous summer evening in the last hour of light. Something about the energy in Madrid kicks us into another gear. We're on autopilot at this point, perfectly in our element, unfazed by any curve ball life might toss our way. We meet three Milanese girls in the hotel lobby. They seem friendly, but no one is keen to strike up a conversation.

We're changed men.

For now.

Weeks of partying will do this.

Our small, charming duplex apartment is designed by a romantic. Above each bed is a glass roof for stargazing, inasmuch as the city skyline here allows. In a different time, on a different day, DJ would have maximized the glass roof's full potential. Cheese fondue and stargazing will make a deadly combo.

Ten years ago, at La Rosa Náutica, Lima, the seafood restaurant that lights up the Pacific Ocean, Justin, Brian, Lulu, DJ, and I shared old memories and looked to the future. Today at Gastrochigre Madrid, a Spanish fusion restaurant near Plaza de Santa Ana, over ramen, fried calamari, mushrooms baked in brie, and other tapas, we gain insights into each other's private lives.

"What's the Wi-Fi?" DJ asks the waitress at Gastrochigre.

We ask each other soul-searching questions that normally have no place on the soccer field or around the beer pong table.

"DJ," I ask, "you miss your girlfriend? I haven't seen you talk to her at all."

"Well, we did talk in Marseille," DJ replies.

"That was like two weeks ago!"

"She's at home in Florida visiting family," he explains.

She is so different from his previous girlfriends. She's more independent, less into nightlife. How exactly they got together, I don't know.

"Do you miss your last girlfriend?" I say, bringing back memory of his tell-all night in Barcelona.

"I wish her happiness," he says, displaying a sentimentality that is almost uncharacteristic.

Kenny chimes in, straight to the point. "DJ, which one of us messed with you the most?"

Monaco, Pamplona, this entire book ... Justin and I have to be the frontrunners.

"No one," DJ says, absolving us all from being bad friends.

"Really?" Kenny looks surprised. "I feel like we made fun of you too much."

"You know," DJ softens his tone, "I don't mind when you guys make fun of me. I'm happy about it sometimes actually; it's a safe place for me to face my shortcomings."

What class.

What a man.

We love our brother of twenty-five years because of who he is. And we love him for letting us make fun of him for who he is.

We then switch over to Dave, who broke up with his long-time girlfriend a while back.

"Dave, you miss you ex?" Kenny asks.

"Well, I wish her happiness too. Hope she gets an upgrade," he smiles. "Don't think she will though."

That's the Dave we know.

.   .   .

Walking home from dinner, Kenny, Brian, and DJ take on Dave in a foot race for one last shot at the belt. Brian injures his hamstring in the process. Kenny and DJ never stand a chance. Dave, as he claimed from the beginning, is going home with the belt.

In an ultimate "wtf" moment, Kenny picks up a six-pack from a convenience store.

"Just in case we play beer pong," he explains.

Alcohol is the last thing on our minds. Needless to say, the beer remains untouched in our apartment refrigerator.

Our journey a decade in the making is coming to an end. A night out in Madrid awaits on this last night, but after all our exploits, we have nothing left. We have partied like the Pitbull rap song "International Love," minus the love. With the AC on full blast, we watch a Bruce Lee movie dubbed in Spanish and take turns with the shower. Then, one after another, we fall asleep. I pop a NyQuil and say my goodnights. I share the bed with Brian once again—my designated bedmate since Paris.

I text Molly about Lupe. They're going camping over the weekend.

"Is she gonna have a backpack?" I ask.

I think I'm ready to go back to my family.

EPILOGUE

THE RUNNING shower downstairs wakes me from my deep, NyQuil-induced sleep. I slept like a baby and could sleep more. Brian is playing with his phone in bed and giving me no attention whatsoever—this after sharing a bed for five nights. What a heartbreaker.

I steal a roll of toilet paper from the apartment for my runny nose. The yellow packet, after all, couldn't save me.

"You took a whole roll of toilet paper? You CB. You gonna take the Bible, too?" These are Brian's parting words to me.

But he's right. That's pretty CB of me. I hope Brian catches whatever virus I have.

"DJJJJ!" Kenny yells from downstairs, "we're going home today!"

"I'm coming home. I'm coming home," DJ sings.

"Guys, I found our next trip," Kenny announces. "You know bubble soccer? Where people are half-encased inside an inflated bubble and play soccer? Introducing—bubble *bull-fighting*."

He shows us a video. His bucket list grows longer every day.

Mom texts me from Ibiza.

The beaches are really beautiful. We swam at one of the beaches yesterday. We have been to nine beaches. Food is great. All restaurants we went to are very good. Not cheap, but not too expensive either. The villa is comfortable though as you said not well maintained. We all slept well. We cooked a great dinner yesterday and used the pool for the first time. It was very enjoyable. You are generous. Angela and Virginia are having a great time beyond what they expected.

Great, I reply.

She posts a photo of the beach at Cala Olivera with the caption "*is this the 7th or 8th beach in two days?*" Even my mom has caught the Instagram bug.

I think about Lovely Laura, Ocean Beach and Neon Party. Those memories seem so long ago now.

We are out on the street with our luggage, making that awkward pause before saying goodbye, a moment I am all too familiar with.

"Brian, you got your Chanel bag?" I ask.

He pads his duffel bag in affirmation.

"Oh shit, I guess we never got to talk about your proposal, right?" Justin lets out a nervous laugh.

I shrug and smile. "It's okay."

He nods, probably reading my mind from my smile.

"I'm going this way," I gesture. "I guess this is goodbye."

We tend to keep our goodbyes crisp.

And just like that, we go our separate ways. They go to Hong Kong; I continue on my solo trek home. When Hollywood eventually makes this book into a movie, this is the moment I would like my character to shed a secret tear.

Justin had planned to spend an extra day with me in Spain, but later decided to take a road trip in the UK with Vincy. So I'm on my own today.

I've been to Madrid before; today I want to explore a new place. I take the train to Toledo.

Coming out of the train station, I hop on a City Sightseeing bus. I have always wanted to try that. We take the scenic route into the medieval city. The bus stops at key lookout points for pictures along the way, which is great for the lazy and impatient traveler in me.

Surrounding the city are aqueducts that pull water a hundred meters up to the city. I don't understand the science behind it, even though I should as a former water-processing engineer.

Toledo is known as the "city of the three cultures" where Christians, Arabs, and Jews have lived together for centuries. I stumble into Santa María cathedral, the second-largest cathedral in Spain. I chance upon Puerta del Sol, a defense tower and city entrance built in the fourteenth century. I would have gone into Alcázar if I had known that it housed the Castilla-La Mancha Regional Library. All told, I visited four museums over three weeks in Europe: the Sex Museum, Erotica Museum, Prostitution Museum, and Heineken Museum. My mother should be proud.

My Toledo walkabout continues in 39° C heat. A young happy couple is getting married at the Monastery of San Juan de los Reyes among friends and family sprinkling them with rice (for fertility) and salt (for abundance). The elegance and simplicity of their ceremony feels refreshing.

My last piece of business in Toledo is to visit FlyToledo.

"Are you a student?" the girl asks, who looks to be college age. "Students get the second ride for free."

"I wish," I reply, handing her a ten-euro note.

Strapped into a harness, I zipline out of the city along San Martín Bridge and end the day on a high note.

Waiting for my train back to Madrid, I soak in the gorgeous view from the Toledo station platform. If I were to paint this, I would start with the clear blue sky. Then, I would trace the golden contours of countryside Spain, adorned with a handful of green trees and country houses. A lone power line would run across the page, maybe with a bird perched on top. I take a deep breath and try to savor the purity of the moment. I feel like a schoolboy waiting for my train back to the city after a summer visiting country relatives. Where's Justin when you want some Jay Chou songs?

I think about our trip to Kenting. On rental electric scooters we cruised along Taiwan's southern coast. We were just moving along the highway at snail speed—forty kilometers an hour, since you asked—with a spring breeze in our face and GoPros strapped onto our torsos. For me, being on the open road with my friends is the epitome of freedom.

For all the joy and life lessons I have taken from soccer, I am most thankful for the friends I have made playing the game.

I look back to our childhood in Hong Kong, walking home from soccer with Brian, eating sour laces and talking about things eleven-year-olds talk about. I think about the pick-up games against adults on Conduit Road, me in my Italy jersey and Justin in his Air Jordans. I think about Lulu splitting his right nipple diving for a save on the concrete ground. I think about making DJ come to our games just to make the numbers. In every stage of our life, soccer has been the foundation of our friendship.

For reasons I don't quite understand, some people find me cold and serious. My girlfriends, especially, have always compared relationships with me to dating a robot.

When I brought my first girlfriend to Hong Kong one Christmas, she said she discovered a more human side of me.

"You're a different person with your Hong Kong friends. I have never seen you smile like this," she quipped, envious. I wonder if my family feels the same.

I am aware of my double standard when it comes to my friends. My obsession with punctuality is bordering on paranoia. People at work know my distaste for meetings starting late or not ending on time. Even outside of work, I arrive half an hour early for everything. Maybe subconsciously I have the most severe case of FOMO (fear of missing out).

But with Brian, DJ, Lulu, Justin, Dave, Sho, and Kenny, their tardiness doesn't bother me the same way. When we set a time to meet for pick-up soccer, I often spend the first hour juggling myself before anyone else shows up.

We don't have many common values; we find ourselves at odds with each other more often than not. But I think these differences are what make them so special to me. I love DJ even when he treats me like a stranger during his single-minded pursuit of women. I embrace Justin's fondness for the limelight. I love Brian knowing that he never messages me just to say hi. Even though Lulu backed out of the trip, I still love him. I miss his contagious laugh. I miss playing pool with him in Hong Kong while shooting the breeze and wagering shots. I miss when he woke up on our third morning in Taipei years ago yelling, "I don't want to go home yet!"

I can be abrasive, self-centered, and intolerant; they all somehow find ways to embrace my imperfections. We are primary school classmates, soccer teammates, partners in crime. Most importantly, we are brothers. I love them to death, even when they are hunched over their phones and don't do chores. When I see them, my heart is filled with joy, even if they are an hour late.

Despite my best efforts, I still missed out on most of our outings. But even when I am not with them in person, I am with them in spirit. I live vicariously through our WhatsApp group chat. There's a framed black and white picture of us from Kenya at my desk. I think about them every day.

Every time they plan a trip, I torture myself on whether to fly halfway across the world to join. These trips take a lot out of you. In Taipei, I lost my voice after the first night. A severe cold crippled me for weeks after.

Was that worth the trouble for three nights?

I offer the same answer now as I did then—yes.

Part of me needed the thrill. I was living in suburban America where the lighting of the town Christmas tree was my year's highlight. Being a Lan Kwai Fong playboy was never my thing, but I wanted to live a little and explore the world with my best friends. I couldn't sit in my living room and watch my twenties go by.

The other part of me—the more romantic part perhaps—believed that friendship, like anything worthwhile, shouldn't be taken for granted. When my Goo-ma moved to the US, she didn't return to Hong Kong for eighteen years. Skype and instant messaging didn't exist in her days. Even the purest of friendships would change under these circumstances. In choosing to begin life anew on a different continent, this was a sacrifice she had to make.

Faced with the same dilemma after college, I followed her path. But I also knew I couldn't give up my friendships. I'm a Hong Kong boy to the core. My friendships and family are what define me. The transpacific flights, the jet lag, and the whirlwind trips are my way of showing that I care.

Maybe, I'm not quite a robot after all.

We came back from our 2006 trip changed in many ways. Justin vowed to stay off hair dye for life and hasn't colored his hair since. Lulu's air travel mishaps taught him a lifelong lesson on punctuality. Brian renewed his determination to lose his virginity. DJ got a new nickname that stuck forever. I discovered my passion for writing.

We grew up in more meaningful ways, too. We were five spoiled Hong Kong boys venturing outside our sheltered lives to see the world. The trip broadened our perspectives outside of top schools and jobs. While some of our failures on the road had been epic, we came home with new ambitions and a whole life to look forward to. *Bring it, world!*

Coming home from Europe this time, we happily returned to our ordinary lives. Kenny returns to his all-consuming job. Justin is finishing his last semester of his MBA and has started job hunting. Brian has gone back into hiding, but still doles out recommendations to expensive restaurants upon request. At thirty, we are beginning to see that sometimes, being ordinary is quite okay.

Except for DJ.

In between jobs, DJ has become an adventure junkie. Besides a trip to Bhutan where he shot a new profile picture, he has also been working as an extra on TV sets.

"No lines. And minimum pay," DJ explained.

DJ is full of adventure and surprises. Maybe he really will work for the World Bank one day.

Sho looks forward to the next Liverpool season with new hope. Dave hung out with Premier League legends Teddy Sheringham and David James in Hong Kong through a company event.

Cristiano Ronaldo lifted the coveted European Championship trophy after a resolute Portugal defeated heavy favorite France. Sir Alex waited at the bottom of the podium to congratulate Nani and Ronaldo like a proud father. Though an injury confined him to only a bit part in the Final, Ronaldo's fifty-one goals in all competitions propelled Real Madrid and Portugal to the apex of European soccer. This is Cristiano at the peak of his power. In my mind, there has never been a Messi-Ronaldo debate—CR7 is the greatest of all time.

When I'm not busy shopping for an engagement ring, I browse the Internet to clear up questions from the trip.

Windmills in the Netherlands are used to pump water for agriculture.

It turns out that Samuel Eells had actually traveled to Dunkirk, New York, not Dunkirk, France. For weeks, I had been wondering as to how a frail fellow as himself could have crossed the Atlantic by boat. It makes a lot more sense now.

I hear from our friends in France. Amandine's Airbnb review finds its way into my inbox.

Gerald was very respectful of the instructions given and the place. We highly recommend him. Privately, they add *"hope to see you again in Lille! Amandine & Ramïn."*

No word from Djibril, though. It reminds me of the saying "if you don't have something nice to say, don't say anything at all."

HBO finally gets back to me about my copyright inquiry.

Hello Gerald. Thank you for contacting HBO with your inquiry and for your interest in HBO. Unfortunately, we will have to decline this request. We do not customarily allow our content to be utilized in this way. –HBO Consumer Affairs.

Dear HBO, I want to write back, *thanks for getting back to me after two months. Good luck taking the belt back from Dave.*

I revel in the ordinary pleasures of my life in the US, watching Lupe grow up. I went to the local supermarket last weekend and found canned herring hidden in the foreign food aisle. I was expecting to relive the gastronomic explosion, but to my despair, it tasted like dried tuna.

"I made few mistakes like that already in Hong Kong," Justin said when I told him about it. "It's nothing alike."

Entering a new decade of our lives, we face unprecedented pressure to grow up. One day, the unrelenting chaos will have to end or, hopefully, just take another form. One day, we'll settle into families of our own. One day, we will no longer serve as the centerpiece of each other's lives. One day, Dave's future wife will toss the championship belt. But whatever the future holds, these memories of our youthful abandon live on. May the next ten years bring more joyful memories.

This is how we will remember the summer of 2016, the year we turned thirty.

BONUS — TOKYO

3 MONTHS AFTER TRIP TO EUROPE

"You look like a Pikachu," I say to Lulu.

"Haha, have you seen what you look like?" he responds.

In a skintight Frieza costume, an impulsive purchase an hour ago, I pose in front of the full-length mirror in our hotel room. *Yes*, I think to myself, *it's a bit revealing.*

We are in Tokyo for Halloween, a spontaneous trip born out of Lulu's breakup. As his four-year relationship came to a close, Lulu needed some company. I was in Asia for work, so Justin, DJ, Brian, and I treated him to beer and bar food at our favorite pub in Wanchai.

"Come join me in Tokyo this weekend," I said.

DJ decided to join on the spot. He had nothing better to do than filling in as TV extras. Justin and Brian couldn't make it, which was understandable.

So here we are in Tokyo, me as a Dragon Ball villain, him as a chubby Pikachu, and DJ a perverted Luigi.

And just like that, we made up with Lulu.

We will give him grief forever for missing the trip, but he will always be our brother.

ABOUT THE AUTHOR

Gerald Yeung grew up in Hong Kong. He loves soccer and travel. His travel stories have been featured in magazines, the Hong Kong government youth blog, and a Travelers' Tales humor collection. These days, he can be found in Northern California. You can follow him on www.geraldyeung.com.

Made in the USA
San Bernardino, CA
07 July 2020

75050576R00173